THE
REDNECK
CEO

FAITH, HOPE &
HARD WORK

GARY A. FINDLEY

PRAISE FOR *THE REDNECK CEO*

"*The Redneck CEO*, the newest book from my longtime friend Gary Findley, will enhance your personal and professional life from the first page turn. Gary's authentic communication style and his wealth of real-world experience are exactly what we need right now.

My advice? Get *Redneck CEO* and read this book immediately. As a global communicator speaking to thousands in person and millions on social media each year, I understand what it takes to develop leaders – from captains of enterprise, to world leaders, celebrities and even the special operations community. We need to hear from more leaders like Gary who are champions for integrity, resiliency and real faith lived out for all to see. *Redneck CEO* is packed with the inspiration to achieve success in these critical areas and more."

- Victor Marx
President & CEO of All Things Possible Ministries and The Victor Marx Group

"A quick, entertaining, and insightful read from a man who has experienced much success, learned from several failures along the way, and above all, held on to his small-town roots and faith in God."

- Dr. Randy O'Rear
President of the University of Mary Hardin-Baylor

Hardcover Publication Date: 2022
Paperback Publication Date: 2022
E-Book Publication Date: 2022

ISBN: 978-1-7347799-5-0 (hardcover)
ISBN: 978-1-7347799-4-3 (paperback)
ISBN: 978-1-7347799-3-6 (electronic)

First Edition Published 2022

BizComPress

A division of BizCom Associates
BizComPR.com
450 Century Pkwy #2
Allen, TX 75013

Printed in the United States of America

CONTENTS

FOREWORD

If you want to assess the character of a man, observe him when he thinks nobody is watching.

In 2011, I had the opportunity to meet Gary Findley at a convention in Las Vegas where I was the opening keynote speaker. The company hosting this convention was a tremendously successful fitness franchise, and I was thrilled to be amongst such a high energy group of entrepreneurs.

Following the program, I walked the tradeshow floor and was approached by a stranger who spent 20 minutes showering me with compliments. He had a thick Texas accent, but what I noticed above all else was his intense focus on me. He asked about my family, honored me for my military service, and was truly appreciative of the impact I made on the attendees.

Little did I know he was the COO of the company and a huge star in the franchise world. He never told me who he was. It was all about me.

Years later, when he re-hired me to speak to his Restoration 1 franchise network, I still met the same man. But this time, he was eager for me to get to know his son and right-hand wingman Micah. I watched him walk the crowd (holding his wife's hand) at the social event, connecting with his employees and franchisees. He knew everyone's name.

That's Gary Findley. Putting others first. Focusing on relationships. Honoring family.

Real, respectful and, yes, a "redneck."

So here I am, ten years later, proudly writing the foreword to his book.

Some may ask, what does a Jewish fighter pilot from New York have in common with a Baptist redneck from a tiny farm town in Texas? Absolutely nothing...and absolutely everything.

You see, believe it or not, we both grew up in similar environments. Gary lived down the street from a dairy farm in a three-bedroom ranch house with just 1.5 baths. I grew up in a similar home on eastern Long Island, except we had only one bathroom for the six of us!

While Gary was feeding cattle, bailing hay, and riding a small 100 cc motorcycle, I was mowing lawns, delivering papers, and riding an 80 cc dirt bike in the woods behind my house. I still remember the peacocks and wild turkeys roaming the neighborhood and the walks to the nearby dairy farm to pick up fresh milk. And, just like Gary, I remember the cow "smell" when the wind blew south.

Finally, I recall parents quite similar to Gary's, who instilled in me and my siblings a foundation of respect, integrity, responsibility, a strong work ethic, and who made sure that God and family always came first. Coincidentally, while Gary's dad was an Air Force veteran, mine served in the Navy. His favorite quote was "Don't take the easy way out!" And that's what The Redneck CEO is all about.

It's a story about how a man from humble beginnings can make it to the top level of business by staying true to his values, integrity, faith, and hard work.

It's about one man's journey through the ups and downs of business and life, where character, relationships, and service are more than just words. They are the building blocks of success - in and out of the business world.

Ultimately, The Redneck CEO demonstrates that no matter where you come from, you can win.

Packed full of heartfelt anecdotes and actionable life lessons on leadership, relationships, and business, it shares the kind of wisdom you can't learn in school. Real world and relevant, it can help everyone from aspiring entrepreneurs, seasoned franchise executives, and everyone in between.

Gary Findley is living proof that when you do the right thing, focus on service, and never sell out for money or pride, success will come. It may not come on your timeline, but it will eventually come.

Let this book shake up your expectations of what defines success and ignites your curiosity. Study its principles and use them as a flight plan to create the life and success you want and deserve.

Let Gary be your wingman just as he has been for me. He'll make you a better leader and most importantly, a better human being.

Never Fly Solo,

Lt. Col. (ret.) Waldo Waldman
Hall of Fame Speaker, Executive Coach, and New York Times bestselling author

DEDICATION

I want to dedicate this book to the most amazing family you could ever ask for. My wife, Kim, has been by my side encouraging me and never holding me back from chasing my dream, even when she probably should have pushed me off a bridge. She has kept our home a home while I was out building a future for our family. We just celebrated our 39th anniversary, but I have been in love with her for more than 41 years. I look forward to many more in our Golden Years.

My kids—Zachary, Whitney, and Micah—have grown to become as amazing as we always knew they would be. They are all special in their own way. They have watched me chase the American Dream while never losing sight of our important and close relationships. We now have additions to the family with Zach's wife, Natalie, Whitney's husband, Andy, and Micah's wife, Meighann. It's awesome to see others who love your kids as much as you do.

Thanks, Mom and Dad, for raising me in a Christian home where I could pass on that faith to my kids and know how to chase a dream.

And, finally, I saved the best for last. To my grandkids, Wyatt, Allie, Emma Harper, Zoe and the ones on the way. They truly make our lives complete.

*"Not every idea is
a good franchise, and
not every franchise
is a good idea."*

– Gary Findley

1

COUNTRY BUMPKIN

It all began in a dusty, rural country town called Axtell, Texas. That was home for me. For the first 17 years of my life, this was what I knew. The people, the places (however few), and the land were what felt familiar. And it wasn't just home. It was a way of life.

If you remember the tale of the country mouse and the city mouse, then I was the country mouse. And this is where I loved to roam.

My whole family loved it, too. Between Axtell, Mount Calm, and Hubbard, three small towns in Central Texas, I can count five generations across both sides of my family who grew up in the area and eventually settled in Axtell. However, for strangers passing through our little bit of heaven between two state highways, you can't blink, or you would miss it. To describe this small town to other people, it's often easier to describe what wasn't there.

A big city to us was a place with a grocery store, a 7-Eleven, a movie theater or even a bigger gas station. Those were all things we didn't have in Axtell. But if we wanted or needed them, we hopped in the car and drove to Waco, a big city by our standards 20 minutes down the road. If you wanted to buy clothes, go out to dinner, see a matinee or any of that stuff, you were going to have to drive to do that.

However, not all was lost. If you did shop in Axtell, you had two places to go. Okay, one-and-a-half if we're being serious. One store in town was 90 percent beer joint and 10 percent sundry. The other one situated just around the corner from where I grew up was an old-time country store. I'm not sure how they perfected the fine art of small-town supply and demand, but they had everything you could ever imagine in there. From cheese, bread, and milk to mousetraps, hardware, and lumber, this little place was our saving grace. It even had an old post office right inside.

We weren't living in the Wild, Wild West exactly. But there's a pretty special story that went around about my grandmother— Allie Crosslin on my father's side of the family—that paints an accurate picture. One day, when she lived in Mount Calm, a car came driving down these old dirt roads in town and right up to her house. The man and the woman in the car stopped and asked my grandmother for some water. She kindly obliged. (We're nice like that in the South. Yes, even to total strangers.) She gave them the water, and they thanked her and drove off. There was nothing special to it at all. Actually, for life in rural Texas, there was nothing unusual about it, either. But as the story goes, these people turned out to be pretty famous strangers named Bonnie and Clyde.

Now, I'm not 100 percent sure if it's true, but that's how my dad and uncle told it. I'll swear that my grandmother lived to the ripe old age of 97 and went to her grave never denying it. That's good enough for me, because that pretty much sums up these rural roads we knew so well—the kind of places famous outlaws might go to hide. But here we were calling it home, and it was the very best kind of upbringing I could imagine. It was small-town life with small-town folks who were friendly...to everyone.

Among the friendly locals in Axtell were my father and mother, Robert Lewis Findley and Doris Findley. They grew up there, went to school there and got married and started a family there. They had two children. My older brother, Robert William Findley, who we all call Bobby, came first. Three years later they had me in October 1961.

To this very day, I consider it a blessing from God that he gave me these parents, this family, this home, and this community to raise me. I lived in the very same house from the day I was born until I was 17 years old and graduating from high school. It was modest by most standards, but it was everything to me. This three-bedroom, one-and-a-half-bath, one-story, brick ranch house put a roof over our heads and was full of love. It sat on a nice piece of land with plenty of room to play, too. I would soon find out that growing up in the country meant the whole town was our backyard.

We lived close enough to the nearby dairy farm, which wasn't hard to guess was nearby when the wind was just right. I can vividly remember the aroma as the cross breeze carried it through my window every day of my early existence. That was just fine by me. Soon enough, animals would become a huge part of my childhood, and that was exactly as it should be. Life at the Findley house was special that way.

I tell people that I loved everything about my childhood, absolutely everything. As far as we were away from the big city, we always had something to do and I never felt alone out there. How could I? For a small town of a few hundred people, I not only knew everyone, but I was related to a lot of them, too. My grandparents, uncles, aunts, and cousins were all just a stone's throw away. I joke that the roads in Axtell were like tic-tac-toe. Four streets ran east and west and three streets ran north and south. On that tiny grid, on every one of those streets, I was related to somebody.

But you know that old saying about keeping things in the family? Well, good luck. Family or not, in my hometown everyone knew your business. That wasn't a bad thing. The community always came together to help when needed. Neighbors really cared about one another. We weren't close enough to wave from the front porch, but you would be surprised how fast word could spread from one house to another. Long before the internet or texting, we had party lines on the telephone where people could easily eavesdrop and learn just about everything going on. I'm here to tell you that small-town gossip was lightning fast. People in my house were always in the know. To say we were a tight-knit community is an understatement. When news traveled fast, it also traveled straight through our front door. That was mostly thanks to my dad, Robert. You see, he was kind of a big deal in our town.

The upstanding positions in our humble city were not what you would expect. Axtell didn't have a mayor or anything. Heck, we didn't even have law enforcement. But there were definitely mentors and leaders around. If you were a leader in our community, you were on the water board. You served on the school board. You coached the baseball teams. You were a deacon or an elder in the church. Those were the people everyone looked up to, and that was my dad. He did all those things and more.

When our Little League team needed a coach, dad volunteered. When the church was fundraising, dad was involved. When the water board was meeting, dad had a seat. And when moms were at our front door to complain about their daughters not making cheerleader, yep, there was my dad from the school board to listen.

As most kids do with their parents, I looked up to this man. In Axtell, Texas, so did a lot of people. Not only was he my personal hero and our family's provider, but he was also a voice of reason for so many others. That also meant that my brother, Bobby, and I were "school board kids." We knew to stay out of trouble. We did, for the most part...or maybe we just didn't get caught. However, life in the country pretty much guaranteed that we didn't get mixed up in anything bad worth mentioning. That's because growing up wasn't slow and easy like others might think. Sure, folks in the big city might have lofty ideas about retiring to the country one day like it's some kind of vacation, but it's not. As far back as I can remember, I kept very busy learning a lifelong lesson that remains with me to this very day. I learned about hard work.

Plain and simple, when you own land, you also have to maintain land. I'm not talking about mowing a front yard in 20 minutes and flipping some switch for automated sprinklers. I'm talking about driving tractors, baling hay, feeding animals, and chopping firewood. These kinds of chores simultaneously become second nature while also building first-class character in small-town folks. I count myself lucky to not only know these people but also to be one of them.

More importantly, that lifestyle serves up an equal dose of hard work while testing one's perseverance on a regular basis. When you're riding your bike and the chain breaks, guess what? You're also in the middle of nowhere. There's nobody to help. You've got to figure things out. When you're on a combine in a field past dusk and the engine cuts off, guess what? You're now a mechanic if you plan to make it out of there.

Problem solving was not just a special gift in the country, it was a requirement. We grew up learning to be resourceful, independent, creative and, most of all, hard working. If you wanted to survive in the country, you learned how to do things. Then you also learned how to fix things, rig things, invent things, and deal with all the things in between to make life happen. You weren't afraid of getting dirty. The daily forecast was hot and sweaty. You had an appreciation for serious labor, which came along with adventure. If life handed you obstacles, it also served up sweet justice when you overcame them. The journey was eternally rewarding.

Others might look at this kind of life and call me a "country bumpkin." Total strangers might think I'm just one of those dumb hicks who likes to kick around in the dirt. That's their definition, not mine. Instead, I'll wear that label with pride, because I can trace my success in life all the way back to the hard work and common sense I picked up in Axtell. It was a breeding ground to harvest one of the most important crops around: responsibility. Every season of my childhood was full of it.

###

A strong runner-up in the character-building book of country life was a sacred appreciation for a strong faith. It was instilled in us from high above, and it was reinforced with churchgoing on a regular basis. Surprisingly, segregation had long gone away, but its churches still remained that way. Lord knows life was colorblind out on the farms, on the ranches, and at school. Half of my friends were African American. But come Sunday, we all ended up at four very distinct churches around our little town, and they were entirely separate but equal. Three of them had African American congregations, and one was for the rest of us. Regardless of your skin color, God expected you to show up at one of them.

I grew up going to Axtell Baptist Church every Sunday morning, every Sunday night, and every Wednesday, too. Good Baptists got right with God in the middle of the week, so we didn't go too long without seeking His direction. My grandparents, Martin "Cowboy" Luther and Eva Luther (on my mom's side), lived right across the street from church. Every church visit was another reason to stop by and see them, too. That ol' church lesson to give a man a fish or teach him to fish was well received. Going out back to fish in the pond behind their house was one of my favorite things to do.

We learned the Golden Rule like we learned to eat and breathe.

We respected our elders, which included the heads of our households and the leaders in our churches. In my case, my dad was both. So for me, being a country boy and being a Christian went hand in hand. If doing chores was routine, so was sitting in a church pew. I was part of a great youth group at Axtell Baptist, where my dad was also a deacon. Being a part of such a strong Baptist community meant you didn't even think about bending the rules. In fact, the only time you didn't show up for church on a Sunday is when you were deathly sick or out of town on vacation. There weren't any other acceptable excuses. It was the law, and so were the rituals at church service. Things were precise. You entered the sanctuary, you grabbed your bulletin, and your next hour on God's green earth was fully scripted. Nothing deviated from what was written on that paper. All the men were in their suits and cowboy boots (my dad had an amazing collection of cowboy boots!), and all the women were in their Sunday best. You just followed that bulletin from beginning to end outlining the service from start to finish, singing the songs verse after verse, and quoting Scripture until it was time to go home and begin a new week. I used to say that if the Holy Spirit wanted to show up and it wasn't in the bulletin, then He couldn't show up. That's how structured church was.

That respect for the church brought order and togetherness to our community. It also planted the seed for my own strong faith that has remained with me ever since. My dad set a great example for me to follow, and I can still appreciate a day of rest for people who live a life of hard, backbreaking work the rest of the week. Beyond that, I knew then as I know now that there is a Higher Power guiding us all. Just how close He had an eye on me was yet to be seen.

###

If I can credit the country life for a great work ethic and church life for my faith, I suppose I have to address what school was like somewhere in all of this. As you might have guessed, my school was small, I mean really small.

We had one school, which to nobody's surprise went by the highfalutin name of Axtell School. It housed grades K-12, and every kid I started with crossed the stage with me our senior year.

I like to tell people that our school was so small, football players would play on the field, take off their shoulder pads at halftime, march in the band, and suit up again to finish the game. We had to learn to do it all because there simply weren't enough of us to go around. I only had 24 students in my graduating class. In fact, I ended up marrying one of them. I'll share more on that later. Anyway, I'm pleased to say that I was in the top half of my class. However, now that you know how small my class actually was, it really wasn't all that hard. I just made better grades than 12 other people. Back then, the mentality was that as long as you were making good enough grades to graduate, that's all you really needed. So, when it came to book smarts, I learned to do enough. Overall, I was uninterested in academics, which made me a wonderfully average "B" and "C" student.

I went to school to be with my friends. I played baseball. I learned welding. I also participated in high school rodeo, competing in bull and bareback riding. That was my kind of school sport. It was pure and crazy fun going to riding competitions. It also reinforced a redneck saying: "You can't fix stupid." There is hardly a lesson that can be learned by riding an animal that only wants to throw you off, but it was just my speed for physical fitness living out in the country. Like life, when you get bucked off, you have to get back on. That would become a theme for me for years to come.

Through it all, I made decent enough grades and kept moving along. Nevertheless, I was never what you would call a "bookworm." That surfaced later in life. Instead, school and overachievement for me meant what I could achieve as soon as school was over. On any given day, I couldn't wait for the bell to ring so I could run home and have some fun.

Now, compared to the big city, there weren't exactly a lot of places to go in town. Then again, we managed to go everywhere as kids. We found adventure by setting out on adventures. When we were looking to have fun, we found it in the great outdoors.

Sometimes that meant I would go home and ride my motorcycle. Before I was old enough to drive, my parents gave me a little 100cc motorcycle for my birthday that I cruised around on. It was the epitome of boyhood. Years later, it would lead to my serious and expensive passion for Harleys. Back then, it was just enough power to keep me occupied. They say there are two kinds of people with motorcycles: those who have had a wreck, and those who will have a wreck. Well, I had one on that motorcycle when I was 15. Luckily, it wasn't bad. So I told myself, "Okay, I got that out of the way," and I just kept on riding...for years and years and years.

Another one of my favorite things to do after school was to saddle up my horse for a different kind of ride. We had horses like other kids have dogs, only these four-legged family members took a lot more time to feed, clean, and care for. Better yet, they also did a whole lot more than fetch. I could ride to town, to the store and, on occasion, to school on my horse. That's right. I was literally on a horse on a paved road like it was Dodge City. Where I grew up, this wasn't out of place. The best thing to do after school was to gallop over to a friend's house, saddle up his horse, and then hit the trails with our buddies. We'd ride and lose track of time until the sun went down and we had to be home for supper.

I had several horses growing up, but one of my most prized possessions was a mare named Coco Barnett. She was a registered thoroughbred who had been on a racetrack for a while, but she wasn't fast enough. Her bad luck on the track was my good luck as a kid. I think it was her size and coloring that I was particularly fond of. She had this very distinctive chestnut color, a silver mane, and silver tail. She was absolutely beautiful and great fun to ride. What's really funny since I'm only 5'7" is how I loved tall horses like her. I'm sure that's because I felt like my idol, John Wayne, sitting on top of her. He always had these big horses, and I had seen every one of his movies growing up. So it's safe to say my horsing around after school was quite literally a little bit of John Wayne reenacting on those trails with my friends.

On other days, we might kick things up a notch and go from cowboy to full-on redneck by going hunting, as we called it. I use the term very loosely. This was the country, so of course we grew up owning guns. But it's not like we had deer or wild hogs all over the place. No, our idea of hunting was actually heading out into the woods, lining up cans, and shooting at them. It was target practice and male bonding at its finest.

There you have it. We played hard and we loved every minute of it. Life was grand when I was a kid. Once upon a time, it included a grand champion, too.

The single most important time that school and fun collided for me, I was 16 years old. That's when a 1,000-pound animal showed me how to conquer big goals. I was participating in Future Farmers of America (FFA) at school that year, a national, intracurricular student organization for agriculture and leadership. This was going to be my blue-ribbon moment. I had decided to go after the biggest of all prizes. I would raise, train, and show a heifer in the cattle show competition. It was a huge commitment of time, patience, and hard work. I was up before dawn to feed and exercise my animal. I spent countless months training, grooming, and caring for this creature as if it was my child, rain or shine. Miss Syria Manso was her registered name, but I called her Siri. I bought her for $200 with money that I had earned. I had friends invest four to five times as much in show cattle that came from high-end breeders. Still, I wasn't intimidated; I was determined.

I raised her from a calf to a heifer and made sure she knew I was her trusted leader. Before long, she overshadowed me and could have crushed me by her sheer size. But instead, she honored my every command.

By the time I was ready to show her in competition, this giant was following me around like a lovesick puppy. She weighed over 1,000 pounds and was under my complete control. She was strong, she was beautiful, and she was crowned the grand champion, the highest honor of the competition. We even had our picture taken at one event that ran on the front page of the *Dallas Morning News.*

It was one of the greatest lessons in my lifetime that hard work pays off. It also showed me that no dream is too big to go after. That's literally and figuratively no bull. When I finished showing her, I sold her. She should have brought a lot of money, but she wouldn't breed. So I sold her to a breeder who used her as a teaser for bulls. I remember earning a couple thousand dollars on that deal and I was walking on clouds.

I can't describe what it was like to have so much money all at once. It was the single biggest payday I'd ever had. I also knew exactly what I was going to do with it. I made the only decision that any good redneck teenage boy could make. I used that money to buy my very first truck—an old Ford F-150 that I tricked out with fancy rims and cherry-bomb mufflers. You could hear me coming from a mile away. That was my ride through the rest of high school. Next to my horse, Coco Barnett, it was my second biggest prized possession.

I had a special kind of love for that truck, unlike anything I had ever worked for before. I felt like I had really earned it. I mean I *really* earned it. This wasn't the result of some quick side-hustle. Some serious sweat, long months, and 1,000 pounds of blue-ribbon power went into that truck.

That brings me to the most important lesson I picked up out in the country: my hunger to be successful. I was never competitive in sports. My brother, Bobby, was the athlete in our family. I only played to have fun. But if there was one thing I was competitive about and determined to win at, it was business. I was downright stubborn about it. If anyone asked me what I wanted to do when I grew up, I already knew.

I wanted to make a lot of money.

Life Lesson: You have the reins. It's up to you where you steer them, regardless of where you come from. When life "bucks you off" – which it will, because there is no such thing as a smooth ride – you have to dust yourself off and get back on.

2

HOMETOWN BOY

What I lacked in interest at school, I more than made up for in ambition. I didn't dream about going off to college. I just wanted to make money, and lots of it. I wasn't surrounded by millionaires. People weren't building mansions around us. But it was in my genes, and I was more than willing to do the work to get there.

If my Boy Scout troop was selling animal feed and the prize was a new BB gun, there was no question I was going to sell the most feed. And I did. If there were odd jobs up for grabs mowing yards around town, I was on it. If there was a way to earn a paycheck before the school day started, my alarm clock was set and I was out somewhere baling hay before morning football practice. In other words, I was working out before I was working out.

When other kids wanted a summer job for spending money, I wanted the summer job that paid the most money. One was always available, because it came at a hot, sweaty, dirty, dusty price. We're talking custom farming in June, July, and August— running combines and plowing fields for farmers in 100 degrees and coming back for more. I once worked for a farmer who had some of the worst equipment you could imagine. In a 10-hour day, I would spend half the time fixing that equipment, which quickly taught me how to improvise. The farmer had one nice tractor that had power steering, required very little maintenance, and was quite comfortable. I learned that if I was the first one there in the morning, I would get my pick of the equipment. Guess who started getting there first? The early bird not only gets the worm, but the best tractor, too.

For extra money on top of that, my friends and I would haul hay in the summer and cut firewood in the winter. It was me, Scott (my best friend who would one day become my future brother-in-law), Dave and Phil (who would become my brother's brothers-in-law and cousins to my future wife). Can you hear the banjos playing? Soon we would all be related somehow. Hillbilly relations aside, the money was good and, just like my grand champion heifer, it always reinforced that hard work pays off.

I'll confess, I still wanted more. I grew up watching the backbreaking, bone-crushing work ethic of rednecks all around me. Soon enough, I was one of them doing those very same jobs. I'll be danged if ambition doesn't have a funny way of turning doers into even bigger dreamers. For this dreamer, I wanted a future with only one title: the boss. I didn't know what I was going to do exactly, but I did know that one fine day my perfect career would bring more than money. I would get to call the shots. I can thank my dad for that.

I was one of the lucky kids. I had a dad who was an entrepreneur.

To be more specific, this was the exception and not the rule for folks in Axtell and our booming population of 600-plus people. The city was founded in the 1880s as a rail stop along the Cotton Belt Railway between Waco and Corsicana. A post office, called Axtell in honor of a railroad officer, opened in 1881. People who settled in the area purposely chose a country life. And not much changed by the time the Findleys came along.

When I was growing up, there was the dairy, the church, the school, some farms – the things you would expect out in the country. If you didn't work at those places, there was one place you probably did work: the General Tire & Rubber Company plant in Waco.

The plant first opened in 1944 when the company, headquartered in Akron, Ohio, decided to open a second location. During World War II, the plant became a huge supplier of tires to the U.S. Armed Forces. As demand grew over the decades, so did plant expansion and the jobs that came with it. By the 1980s, the Waco business stretched across 49 acres under a single roof on 139 acres of land. A big chunk of Axtell's residents were inside there, punching a clock and making a living.

Sometimes that came with the graveyard shift. I had friends whose parents would clock in at 11 p.m. and get off at 7 a.m. Shift work was a way of life for a lot of people in Axtell, and God bless them for their loyalty in doing incredibly hard and monotonous work. They were blue-collar to the bone and I never looked down on that.

Then there was my dad. He was a U.S. Air Force veteran and, as I shared before, a real leader in our community. I saved the best for last because, most importantly to me, he was his own boss. He was a small-business owner and ran Jack's Stereo with his cousin in Waco. This was in the heyday of 8-track tape decks and cassette players with all the latest bells and whistles that people wanted for their cars. As we grew up, my brother and I would sometimes work there on the weekends to help out. Bobby liked being in the back where the installations would happen, and I loved being up front at the counter working with customers where the sales were made. It foreshadowed the skills I would sharpen for my future, and I saw firsthand the upside of owning a business. That made life at the Findley house pretty good, too.

Couple my dad's line of work with my mom, Doris, who worked as a buyer at Cox's, one of the nicest department stores in Waco. Together they were the sharpest-dressed couple around.

My dad was one of the few white-collar workers I knew and, compared to others, that came with a great amount of freedom. He never missed a single baseball game, football game, rodeo event, or you name it. When my brother and I were growing up, if we were participating in something, both of my parents were sure to be there. He was my role model for success, not only because of what he did at work, but also because of what that allowed him to do outside of work. This didn't make us the Beverly Hillbillies, but we were certainly comfortable. We never wanted for anything. That's a heck of a lot more than I can say for others in my hometown.

To be fair, there also wasn't this big contrast between rich and poor in Axtell like you find in bigger cities. Our town wasn't even big enough to have a so-called bad side. But the Findley house was one of those that had some of the nicest cars in the driveway. My mom and dad always had a Lincoln or Cadillac. We always had a boat. We owned a camper, too, and we always made time for family vacations. You know what stood out about that? Nobody had to ask for time off. My dad was his own boss and just did what we wanted.

Ninety percent of our travel was to Colorado. We would drive and camp in different spots, such as the Royal Gorge in Canyon City, and Pikes Peak and Garden of the Gods in Colorado Springs. We had the best times up there. When we got older, we could even bring friends. Growing up that way made an impression on me. I eventually realized I needed to have that same kind of freedom in my future, too.

There it was. I had my plan. I needed to find a way to make a lot of money, and I needed to find a way to be my own boss. As the saying went, I could run with the big dogs or stay on the porch. I was never good at staying on the porch, not even when I probably should have. My plan was a little rough around the edges; I wasn't one for details just yet. First, I needed to finish high school. Quite frankly, this was about the time that it came with a wonderful little distraction: Kim Turner.

As fate would have it, I honestly can't say that I found the girl of my dreams, because it's the God's honest truth that my future mother-in-law found me first. Cue the hillbilly music here, folks. This story is a keeper.

It was June 1978. I was 16 years old, and my brother was getting married to Cassie, a great local girl whom he had dated for a long time. If there's one thing that Southerners will travel for, it's a relative's wedding. It just so happened that Cassie's aunt, Kathleen Turner, came all the way from Arizona to attend the ceremony. Well, wouldn't you know it? Here I am in my suit, looking the part of a handsome groomsman. I can't tell you squat about the vows they exchanged. I'm not even sure I listened to the pastor. What I can tell you is that I had a great time at Bobby's wedding. Pretty much any time I'm around a crowd of older adults, it's like an open invitation to entertain them. My redneck charm goes a long way with the right crowd. I'm not sure where it comes from, but the older my audience, the more I love to tell stories, crack jokes, and help everyone else have a ball. That's just what I did at that wedding, and Aunt Kathleen apparently had a blast.

I'm all about making a good first impression, but I didn't know until later that Kathleen went back to Arizona and told her 15-year-old daughter, Kim, "I just met Bobby's brother. I just met your future husband." No lie.

This teenage girl thought her mother had lost her marbles. To hear it now sounds just shy of crazy to me, too. We were only kids, but somewhere between the "I dos" and cutting the cake at my brother's wedding, there was a woman in the room planning another one.

Six weeks later, the whole Turner family moved from Arizona to Axtell.

I can't take any of the credit for that decision, of course. That whole I-met-your-future-husband stuff was true, but so was the fact that Kathleen's husband, my future father-in-law, was seriously injured while working in an Arizona copper mine. He was disabled and couldn't work, and like so many other dedicated blue-collar people I've known, had a rough life that kept getting rougher.

The light at the end of this tunnel, however, came with a Texas-size invitation. Time and time again, country folks will step up to help out their loved ones when they need it most, and that's what happened here. Kathleen's brother, Keith Hull—if you're following along, he was also my brother's new father-in-law—had some land in Axtell with an empty trailer on it for the Turners to move right in. He told them to pack up, move on down to Axtell, and live there for free. It was a done deal.

Kim had all kinds of ideas about what moving to Texas would be like. Sure, her mom had talked it up. Apparently, she had even talked me up. Plus, everything's bigger in Texas, right? This is when "Dallas" was the top-rated show on TV, the whole world followed J.R. Ewing, and big-time oil money was everywhere. Leaving a poor coppertown in Arizona seemed easy.

Six weeks later, they pulled up to a trailer they were now going to call home in a town that seemed to be in the middle of nowhere. Reality sunk in like a steamy Texas cow patty. There was nothing glamorous about this place. Life had been hard in Arizona, and it was going to be just as hard in Axtell, but they weren't going to face it alone. Now they had a supportive family around them. A new friend named Gary would soon be coming around, too.

The first time I ever met Kim, she walked up to me at school and made fun of me for wearing my jeans tucked in my boots. She found that extremely odd until I explained to her that I had been out in the pasture feeding animals that morning. I wasn't about to show up at school with mud on the bottom of my jeans. By "mud," I didn't mean or say "mud." Isn't that romantic?

Here was this pretty new girl in town. We were both starting our junior year of high school. The very first conversation I ever had with the girl I would one day marry was about cow poop. We were destined to be together.

Before too long, we were together all right, only I wasn't hanging around Kim so much as I was hanging around my new best friend – her brother, Scott. From the time the Turners rolled into town, Scott and I started hanging out every single day. He was at my house, I was at his house, and we did everything together. His two cousins, Dave and Phil Hull, whose dad owned the land and the trailer where the Turners now lived, were always around, too. That became my new posse. Scott, Dave, and Phil were now my closest friends. Without any master plan, that put me smack dab around Kim all the time. It was innocent enough...at first.

I had another girlfriend at the time, but she was only a freshman and not allowed to date yet. When you're a teenage boy out in the country with nothing to do, unless you go out and do something, that means one thing. I supposedly had a girlfriend, but we couldn't go anywhere or do anything. When Scott and I went out, we couldn't double date because my girlfriend wasn't allowed. Instead, I would tag along and, somewhat awkwardly, so would Kim. We were all just a bunch of friends, but who was

I kidding? There was no denying she was the prettiest girl I had ever seen.

Circumstances changed real fast when I started spending so much time at the Turners' place. It was this big stretch of land a few miles down the road from me with three trailers on it. One of them was where the Turners lived. Kim and Scott's uncle (also Dave's and Phil's dad), a preacher and former Air Force pilot, bought the land when he left the military. He built a runway on the property, started a program called the Wings for Christ, and out of the kindness of his heart taught missionaries how to fly for free, as long as they committed to using their time for missionary work.

The only work us kids did on that land, however, was swim, swim, swim. The place had a tank—that's what we call them in Texas—a small, man-made lake. We ended up stretching a halon wire out across the middle, added a trolley from the trees and built a platform. We spent hour after hour jumping out of those trees and swimming in that tank, having the time of our lives. That's also where I first kissed Kim.

Was it a sign from above that I found a real angel, and my one true love, on the same stompin' grounds as the Wings of Christ flight school? Not quite. As far as Kim was concerned, it was a sign that I was a bit more of a bad boy for flirting with a girl when I actually had a girlfriend. We knew we both liked each other, but she quickly informed me that stringing two girls along wasn't the Christian thing to do. I needed to pick one. It was a no-brainer. I picked her.

I drove Kim into Waco for our first "real" date. No brother or best friend was in tow. No double date was kicking this off. For once, it was just me and Kim. We were finally going out as boyfriend and girlfriend. I took her to a restaurant called La Fiesta, which is still there to this day. We settled into a corner booth and ordered our dinner. Everything was going great until the food arrived. I watched Kim devour hers in minutes. Here I thought we were going to take it slow, chat, eat, flirt, and make a real occasion of this. You know, like a real date. But she ate, looked up and said, "Okay. You ready?" I was only midway through my meal, but I decided to be a gentleman. Even though this was some of the best Mexican food in town, I wasn't going to make her sit there and watch me keep eating. Here I was dating this girl I really liked, and I wanted her to like me, too. I said, "Okay," and we walked off. I left my first date with Kim both totally infatuated and completely hungry. I laugh about it now, but that dinner was the icebreaker that helped us find our stride. Within no time, we felt comfortable as a couple.

My junior and senior years of high school went from good to great now that I had my high school sweetheart. To this day, I tell everyone that I out punted my coverage with Kim. This beautiful blonde from Arizona was way out my league, and I was one lucky redneck. I was lock, stock, and barrel in love. So much so that her mom's prediction about us one day getting married didn't seem so bizarre after all. As I looked past high school graduation, I couldn't exactly see my future, but I also couldn't see living without Kim.

As we grew closer to one another, I shared my dreams about wanting to be successful and spending the rest of our lives together. When we went into Waco on dates, we would drive past this big house that looked like an antebellum home out of a storybook. I would tell Kim, "One day I'm going to make a lot of money, and I'm going to buy you that house." She would just smile.

She had gotten to know me pretty darn good and had a front-row seat to my ambition – both my desire to make money and my stellar ability to spend it. We tell people that she has always been the saver and I've always been the spender. When you've barely crossed the graduation stage, that's not a recipe for walking down the aisle next.

In 1980, right after graduation, Kim worked for an insurance company. I still hadn't figured things out, but push came to shove. I kept pushing the thought of marriage, and she shoved me right out of our relationship. I was totally and utterly crushed. I can look back now and see she was the voice of reason when she said we were still too young. Honestly, what were we going to do? How were we going to live? I didn't have those answers.

Right when Kim and I broke up, one of her brothers, Danny, broke up with his girlfriend, too. How's that for a happy graduation? One of my best friends and I were now jilted bachelors, diving headfirst into summer with nothing on the horizon. We decided to lick our wounds, put Axtell in our rearview mirror, and vowed to never look back. But where would we go? The only other place Danny had ever lived was in Arizona. That sounded as good as anywhere else, so we packed up my car and headed west. We were going to ride out in a blaze of glory, never to be seen from again. We were back in three days.

Running away from heartbreak wasn't going to fix anything. What I really needed was focus. I was a recent high school graduate in rural Texas. I wasn't ready for college, but I was eager to find a job — the kind of job that paid more than minimum wage. Little did I know that I was going to tackle some of the most backbreaking work of my entire life.

I had an uncle at the railroad, and he said they were starting a rail gang to lay new rail between Waco and Hillsboro that summer. I smelled a hot opportunity. I applied and he put in a good word for me. The next thing I knew, I was officially hired by the MKT Railroad. While the rest of the kids in my neighborhood were laying out by the swimming pool, I was with guys laying railroad ties from Waco to Hillsboro and from San Marcos to Lockhart in the prime Texas heat. It was one of the hardest things I had ever done, but I learned three powerful, incredibly valuable things. I've carried them with me ever since.

1. Dirty jobs teach character. There's a reason why some of the most successful people I've ever known have worn overalls in their lifetime. The fact that dirty jobs are necessary puts these people in high demand. The pay that comes with those jobs reinforces why it's more than okay to make it a career. It didn't take long for me to see why laying railroad ties put more money in my pocket than sacking groceries. Ever since then, I've learned to evaluate a good business opportunity by the people who show up to tackle tough jobs that other people would rather avoid. People with character do the jobs that pay well.

2. Learning new skills delivers rewards. We worked some long, grueling hours on the railroad, but I decided to come early and stay late, even on the hardest days. I figured that if I hung around long enough, I would get to do more than just lay railroad ties. When the boss taught me how to drive the Speed Swing loader – the equipment that took up and laid down the rails – those extra skills paid off. One day, when the normal Speed Swing operator wasn't able to come to work, I got to assume his job sitting in the cab of this massive piece of equipment. Here I was with a fan blowing on me, out of the direct sun, managing the crew. I learned in an instant that there is room to move up, even in a world of dirty jobs.

3. The best respect is earned respect. When I transitioned from working alongside my friends to becoming a machine operator in the Speed Swing, I got more responsibility, more pay, and a step up toward management. It could have gone seriously wrong for a teenager with a bit of authority to suddenly have more power than his buddies. Instead, it worked out surprisingly well because I had already walked in their shoes. I didn't ask anything of others that I hadn't already done myself. They respected me for that. To this day, I embrace seeing a business from all levels, even the ground floor of operations, in order to fully understand how work gets done.

Once again I was reminded that hard work pays off. I learned firsthand that some of the best business lessons don't require a coat and tie. In this case, they just required railroad ties.

I kind of knew going into it that it was going to be a short-term gig. I did a stretch in Central Texas for a few months, then I did a stretch farther south outside of San Marcos for a few months. I could have signed up for more, but I had been gone long enough. If you've ever watched "Deadliest Catch" on TV, I was like a crabber in Alaska for high season, but Texas-style. I was only 18 and doing a tough job for a short run for some big cash. And, boy, the money was good. It was also the longest time I had ever been away from home. I had been traveling and staying different places, and now I was ready to head back.

It was an incredible experience. The town that had raised me on the value of hard, dirty, rewarding work was the perfect internship for what the railroad taught me as an adult. I was a little wiser in many ways. In other ways, I still had my favorite habits: Now that I had some cold, hard cash in my pocket again, I also had an urge to spend it.

When I headed home, I stopped short of Axtell and moved to Waco instead. Life as a local yokel was over. As much as I loved Axtell, I was ready for something a little different. When I arrived, I did it in style. I said goodbye to my truck and bought a new, red Z28 Camaro with T-tops and a silver interior. It was my dream car and probably the nicest-looking car in Waco, too. My brothers-in-law still talk about that car.

Here's how rare it was. About once a month, I'll go to every website I can find to search for old Z28 Camaros and I can never find that one. You'll see red ones with silver stripes, but you'll never see one like I had. It was so unique with that silver interior. I loved being in that driver's seat.

Life seemed different all of a sudden. I was a little older, I was living in the big city (by Axtell standards), and I had the best car on the road. I felt like I had officially arrived. There was just one little problem. I needed a job to keep it all going.

###

Life Lesson: Make hay while there's sunshine. Always strive to do your best, no matter the job or task. There is always opportunity for moving up, but opportunities are what you make of them. Regardless of the old adage about opportunity that comes knocking, I've learned you have to be the one out doing the knocking.

3

MOVING ON UP

There's a saying out in the country. Pigs get fed, but hogs get slaughtered. I had no idea that I was about to get an up-close and personal look at how that applied in business and in life, but it would be a humdinger. I would enter a new line of work, meet my first official future billionaire, see the rise and fall of a so-called giant, and do something incredibly fun and then equally painful by deciding to go into the fitness business. My future was about to get a serious workout.

When I first started calling Waco home, I put a few days in here and there by working at my dad's stereo business, which he now called Sound Cellar. Then I immediately began looking for job openings that piqued my interest. I was driving my dream car around town, living off my money from the railroad, and looking for my next serious gig. If something caught my eye, I was going to give it a try. That's when I heard about a job for a trainer at Total Fitness, which was one block down the street. I applied for the job, and I got it.

Before you go thinking that I was some fancy personal trainer, this job title had a completely different meaning in the 1980s. All I did in the beginning was pick up weights, vacuum the carpet, clean the hot tub and swimming pool, and wash members' clothes. If I was training to do anything, it was to be a maid. Nonetheless, I brought some very attractive additional skills. I had become such a good problem solver on heavy equipment out in the country that I could now tackle a broken sauna, solve issues with the pool equipment, or fix the weight machines like nobody's business. On top of that, I got to serve a whole new kind of crowd — very successful white-collar businessmen. That was all the incentive I needed.

Total Fitness was an all-men's health club that was almost like a country club. The guys had their own lockers with their names on them. They would leave their workout stuff there with these oversized clothespins with their locker number on it. They would throw that in a basket and we would wash everything, dry it, fold it, and put it back in their lockers so it was clean when they returned. It was a concierge service at its finest with the facilities to boot.

This club had workout machines, free weights, a hot tub, sauna, steam room, outdoor running track, and a huge indoor swimming pool. The guy who built the place was such a fan of scuba diving that he had the indoor pool made extra deep so he could have a place to practice diving.

We had a masseuse on staff, there were people to guide your workout, and then there were the sales guys. The salespeople were the engine that made everything else possible, and this would be the place where my rookie sales skills would be put to the test.

By the look of so many members in the club, business was pretty good. Keep in mind, I had been a country boy my whole life who went outside and tackled hard labor to earn a little money. Now I was in a place where people freely opened their wallets and paid top dollar to work up a sweat. It was a real light-bulb moment.

At Total Fitness, men paid $1,000 to join. They had these financing programs paying $80 or $90 a month with an annual service fee of another $60. To a kid like me, this wasn't chump change. Quite honestly, it looked more like a cash cow. When it came to selling memberships at those prices, I learned firsthand how to finesse the fine art of high-pressure deals.

We had these sales rooms at the club with two-way speakers that sat on the desk. The manager would sit in his office and listen to this presentation. If it looked like you weren't going to close the deal, he magically walked in to save the day. It was like watching somebody sell a car, old-school style. I found that I had a real gift for growing memberships. I became fascinated with this side of the business. It was a little like working with customers at the front counter at my dad's business, only with a much bigger price tag.

At both places, we were addressing a want and not a need. People didn't need car stereos or cassette players, but lots of them wanted to buy them. Thank goodness they did. My dad did a heck of a job raising a family on that business model.

People didn't need to join a health club, either. Not to mention, there were certainly cheaper places in town to exercise. But Total Fitness really stood out. If you wanted the best and you could afford it, you were a member at our club. The high-end amenities, the first-class service, and that VIP culture went a long way in supporting and growing that business model. I could only imagine what kind of living my new employer was making.

The brains behind the business was a guy named Allen Stanford. He grew up in a little town outside of Waco called Mexia. He was a college student at Baylor University in Waco when he got a job working at a gym called Mr. and Mrs. Health. He fancied himself an entrepreneur, learned the business from the ground up, and had ambitions to make it better. That's when Allen somehow managed to buy the club from its original owner and renamed the place Total Fitness. He totally reinvented the business and packaged himself into a local success story along the way.

Here was this kid who was going to college, working and running a health club at the same time, and then sleeping there at night. The hard work seemed to pay off. As the business grew, so did Allen's reputation around town. By the time I had started working there, Allen had opened locations in Temple and Killeen, with plans to add two more health clubs in Houston and Austin. I'll never forget the first day I met him.

I was vacuuming the carpets at the club one afternoon when I heard this strange noise. I couldn't figure out what it was, so I cut off the vacuum and went over to the window. Right before my eyes, landing in the middle of our running track outside, was this flashy white helicopter with a Total Fitness logo on the side.

This mammoth of a man stepped out. He was all of 6-foot-6, around 260 pounds, and every bit of him was muscle. I remember thinking he had hair like Mr. Brady on "The Brady Bunch." As this giant walked up to the door, I turned and asked my manager, "Who's that?" He said, "That's Allen. He's the owner."

From the first time I met Allen, he was this larger-than-life character. Everything about him looked like money. It wasn't just the helicopter, although that certainly got people talking. He also cruised around in a Jaguar. He had two huge Rottweilers as pets. He lived in a big house, which I visited a couple of times. He seemed to have it all. To me, he was like a Texas version of Tom Selleck from "Magnum P.I." on TV. You didn't just admire Tom Selleck. You wanted to be him.

I told myself that if Total Fitness was doing this well for Allen, then I was in the right place. I was going to be the best at everything I touched at work. Within two months of starting that job, I was promoted to assistant manager. A couple of months after that, the manager got fired and I was suddenly running the place. I was barely 20 and managing the best health club in Waco, and I was killing it on the sales side, too.

That's when Allen started asking me to drive to Austin and Houston to do presales for those grand openings. The more I got to know him, the more I was convinced he was living the dream. And then I got a rude awakening. While he was enjoying all his expensive toys, I got a notice that the pool chemicals had not been paid. Then a string of collection notices started rolling in. The next thing you know, this is overdue and that is overdue. While he made it look fast and easy, serious trouble was brewing.

I showed up to work one day only to find out that Allen had declared bankruptcy.

Everyone was stunned. He had just opened some of these clubs and portrayed himself as sitting on top of the world. Right after that, members walked up only to find the doors locked at those new locations. The Waco club never closed, but nobody had a clue what had happened. People were blindsided.

How could he be broke? I was managing the highest-performing club and watching all this money come in. Where had it all gone? It turned out that for every dollar Allen was making, he was spending $20. The business was good, but his life of luxury was also too good to be true. Being as young as I was, I was no financial genius. But I was smart enough to look at what these clubs were probably making and questioned whether he was living beyond his means.

I was just a redneck from the country. What did I know? The helicopter, the Jaguar, the Rolex, the businesses... I had never seen anything like that. The prized pig everyone was feeding called Total Fitness had turned into a hog that was about to be slaughtered. And these were just the early signs of his reckless business practices. He would go on to do far worse things in life. If I learned one thing from Allen Stanford, it was this: Never spend money quicker than you make it. It made me realize that my integrity was way more important than any amount of money.

The next time I saw Allen, he was over in Hewitt, a suburb of Waco, trying once again to reinvent himself. This time he opened a little burger joint called Juniors Hamburgers. I'll be darned if this place wasn't hopping. The guy was a freaking genius. His name wasn't Junior. He didn't know a Junior. But here was this place where the menu had this whole story about Junior. And the food was good. I saw him in the back at the grill cooking burgers, and I told myself he might be eating a helping of humble pie, too. But the place closed down a little later. Once again, it couldn't have been because he wasn't making money. More likely, he got run out of town because he owed too many people.

His bad management, however, didn't make me love the fitness business any less. I had found a passion for the service industry. So as the clubs went belly up, I went head first into finding a way to buy my location. The country boy decided to take the bull by the horns and figure out a way to keep it going.

My dad had become a fan of Total Fitness in Waco, so he and I approached the trustee overseeing the assets in the bankruptcy. My dad signed the note and we were now co-owners of the original location on Lake Air Drive. I had gone from trainer, to assistant manager, to manager, to business owner in record time. I graduated from wage earner to bill payer. I was 20 and I now owned my own health club. I had reached the ultimate goal I set for myself back in Axtell as a teenager. I now had a way to make money and be my own boss. Or, at least I thought I did. It was full-steam ahead.

My first order of business was to get right with the vendors that Allen had stiffed. As soon as I could, I paid the overdue bills. I still needed those relationships if I wanted to keep my gym going. And go we did.

With a little Findley luck and being in the right place at the right time, I had a bit of a meteoric rise. My work had also become my life. My social situation, however, was a totally different matter, and Kim was never far from the picture. I had dated other girls after high school and she had dated other boys, but it was never anything serious. Plus, her brother Scott and I were still the best of friends, and I lived with her other brother, Danny. So she and I would run into each other on occasion. While we kept our distance, she knew exactly what I had been up to every step of the way. Then one day as I walked to my car outside the club, I found this note stuck on my windshield from Kim. "If you want to do lunch sometime, call me."

We both needed to find ourselves and do a little growing up after high school. I guess by the look of things, we had done that. We went to lunch the very next day and never stopped seeing each other again. That was in June 1982. By September 4, we were married.

The whole topic of marriage wasn't my doing. It had been too stressful before, and after I left for the railroad, I never mentioned it again. But I knew it was only a matter of time. In fact, in high school I told Kim, "I'm going to marry you one day, because God told me." She said, "You better tell God he better get his wires straight, because he didn't tell me that."

One month after we got back together, it was raining one night and we were just hanging around at my place when Kim said, "Let's go to the mall and look at wedding rings." It happened just like that. I guess God got his wires straight. And, of course, I said okay.

We went to the mall, looked at wedding rings, I bought her one, and we got married a couple of months later. Back then, people weren't throwing these elaborate weddings. You didn't propose on a scoreboard in front of the world, plan some big event, and break the bank for a one-day extravaganza. Instead, you just talked about it, you got a ring, and the next thing you know, you're engaged and then you're married.

Kim wanted to make it easy for everybody, so she looked for the next holiday weekend that her relatives could travel from Arizona. We got married on Labor Day weekend at Highland Baptist Church in Waco. It was a proper Baptist ceremony, which means no drinking was involved. We weren't legal drinking age anyway. She was only 19 and I was 20. We said our vows, had cake and punch, and flew to Puerto Vallarta for a short honeymoon. It was official. We were hitched.

Our life started out grand. I had the business and we had each other. Kim also had a job working at Success Motivation International (SMI) in Waco, where I picked her up every day after work. This place had been founded by Paul J. Meyer, another well-known entrepreneur in town. He became a world-renowned motivational speaker and pioneer of the personal development industry. He went on to become not only a successful businessman but a millionaire and philanthropist, too.

When I would wait in the lobby to pick up Kim, the place was like a scene out of "Mad Men." The women were secretaries, and the men were smokers and high-pressure sales guys in suits. Who knew that sitting in that lobby so often would one day lead to a special invitation from the man himself? Paul Meyer eventually asked me over to his home for lunch and became a mentor whom I highly admired for his accomplishments. His power to motivate others was unshakeable. In fact, there was a giant quote on the wall that I would read every day as I sat and waited for my new bride to get off work. It said: "Whatever you vividly desire, ardently imagine and enthusiastically act upon will inevitably come to pass." – Paul J. Meyer

I memorized that quote, I repeated it to myself, and I thought about it on too many occasions to ignore. Something about it spoke to me, and it has motivated me to act on many things throughout my life ever since, starting with when I decided to leave the health club.

The dream of being a business owner and the reality of being a business owner were suddenly no longer one in the same. As much fun as I was having with the health club, things started to get a little complicated. My dad sold his stereo shop and my parents started officing out of the health club. That's right about the time they started to have opinions about the place. I couldn't blame them. We were an entrepreneurial family; it was in our genes. But I also couldn't agree with them.

Coming from retail backgrounds, they started viewing and treating the health club like a retail business. And what do you do in the retail business? You cut costs and you raise prices. They were all about cutting costs. That meant we had all of these happy members at the club who were used to getting certain services, and then we started taking things away. I didn't come from a retail background. I came from a service business. I saw the writing on the wall. I instantly knew this wasn't how I wanted to run things and it wasn't going to end well. I also knew the organization didn't need multiple bosses. However, I didn't vividly desire, ardently imagine or need to act upon things any longer. As much as I loved the club, I loved my family more. Three years into the journey, I decided I needed a change. I left the club to my dad and I got my real estate license.

The club later closed, and it was best that I wasn't there when it happened. I had no hard feelings about it. In fact, I had learned a lot. Plus, there was one transferrable skill I took with me that proved invaluable in the real estate world: my gift for sales.

As a Boy Scout, I could sell enough feed to win the BB gun. At my dad's business, I could sell car stereos that would make driving fun. At the health club, I could sell memberships that would transform you, body and soul. But I was about to hit the big time. I was about to sell everything to people, including the kitchen sink. I was about to sell houses.

In the 80s, after I got my real estate license, I started working for the largest real estate company in Waco, Jim Stewart Realtors. Jim was an elder at our church, Highland Baptist, where Kim and I had gotten married, and we knew his daughter. When I went to work there, they had three satellite offices around town, and the biggest office was in a place called Meadowlake Center off Highway 6 where they focused on residential real estate. Talk about being out of my element. When I walked in there, I counted more than 20 women, all Realtors, and all at least 10 years older than me. I first arrived and they kind of looked me up and down and wondered what this kid was even doing there. Back in the early 80s, I was definitely entering a woman's world. Guys usually sold commercial real estate and women sold houses, but I wasn't about to let that determine my future. I was there to do what I do best, and by the second month, I had the most sales in the office. Once I had that really good run, the ladies started warming up to me. They would ask me to do open houses for them. So that's what I did. I started doing open houses, the money was good and we rode that pony hard for a couple of years. There's a saying out in the country to "ride that horse like you stole it." And I was at full gallop.

Kim and I had been living in a duplex when we got pregnant with our first child. The timing was right because, if I was good at selling houses, it was about time we bought one, too. Kim had seen this cute house for rent that was close to our church, but it needed a fresh coat of paint and new carpet. She didn't want to do all of this work on a home we wouldn't actually own. But the owner, who had been living on that monthly income, was an elderly woman who lived just down the street. So, Kim asked her if she would be interested in selling it. She said, "Only if I can carry the note." Imagine that. She was so used to that monthly check, that this was the only way she would negotiate. That was better than good to us.

We paid $27,000 for our first house. It was a small pier-and-beam home with about 1,000 square feet. Years later, we bought a Chevy Suburban for $32,000 and joked that it cost more than our first house. But back then, the location, the size, and the price were perfect to move in and bring a baby into the world. Eventually my brother-in-law bought the house next door. You couldn't keep us country boys apart.

I was out showing a house one night when Kim actually went into labor. She was at her mom and dad's house at 8 or 9 o'clock when she called to tell me the baby was coming. Always the salesman, I said, "Okay, I'm showing a house. Have your parents take you to the hospital and I'll meet you up there when I'm done." That was Feb. 28, 1984, and when I was done, I rushed over to the hospital. Our son Zachary was born at 12:01 the next morning. We had ourselves a Leap Year baby.

Things were swimming right along when the strangest thing happened one day. I got a call from a guy who wanted me to work for him. That had never happened to me before. I was the one who always went out and looked for a job. On top of that, I already had a job. In fact, I had a really good job. But the offer from this guy was way too hard to resist. He was a real estate developer in town who had put together a subdivision of brand-spanking-new patio homes. I had earned a reputation for being really good at selling houses. He wanted me to help him sell those in his subdivision. On top of that, I could move my family into one and live there for free.

Never in my life had I lived in a new house. The chance to give that to Kim and the baby was the icing on the cake. Just like that, I quit my job, we sold our house, and I started working for my new boss. It was 1985 when we made this smart decision. Right after we did, the real estate market bottomed out. Our world came crashing down. Here I was living in a real estate development with new houses all around me, and I couldn't give them away. The well had run dry. My boss was nice enough to keep letting us live there, but even this country boy knew that would only go so far.

When the real estate market started collapsing, I remember getting a little nervous about my career choices for the very first time. Maybe I should have gone to college after all and gotten a professional degree and done something different. It wasn't like I would have become an accountant or anything. I never liked numbers unless they were on green paper in my hand with a president printed on them. I began to question if a college degree would help. I didn't have time to dwell on it though, because that's right when our car got repossessed. No, it wasn't my red Z28. I wasn't a bachelor anymore. When I picked up a wife and a kid and started showing real estate, we also picked up a Mazda 626. It said I was a full-fledged adult right up until the bank thought otherwise and kindly took it back. There wasn't a single minute to mull over what I hadn't accomplished. I needed to focus on what I was going to do.

As quick as things took a turn for the worse, I had to admit that I didn't lose any sleep over it. I just did what came naturally to me. For a country boy, when things got harder, you worked harder. It was that simple.

That's when I found a future in franchising.

Life Lesson: *Ride that horse like you stole it. When the opportunity arises, make the best out of it. It may not come along again, but don't get greedy. There comes a time when you need to find where your true skills lie and focus on those.*

4

FRANCHISING 101

Since I hadn't gone to college — well, not yet anyway — God smiled down on me in my time of need and decided I should get seriously schooled in a little thing called franchising. Following my recurring pattern of never having a solid plan but always landing in just the right place at the right time, I got involved with an organization headquartered in Waco called The Dwyer Group. The company known as Neighborly today is a global franchise organization with 29 home service brands and 4,800 franchise owners doing more than $3 billion (yes, billion!) in annual system-wide sales. You may know many of their household names like Mr. Rooter Plumbing, Glass Doctor, Mr. Handyman, Mr. Electric, The Grounds Guys, Aire Serv Heating & Air Conditioning, and Molly Maid. Back then, there was only one game in town. I happened upon a ground-floor opportunity with the organization's very first franchise network called Rainbow International Dyeing & Carpet Cleaning. The business had launched in 1981, and its founder, Don Dwyer, was about to become my next brush with profoundly serious white-collar success. He drove a Rolls Royce, flashed a Rolex, wore the suits, and had all the window treatments of a fine life, including a beautiful home, a loving wife, and six kids. I knew he wasn't another Allen Stanford. Allen's vision for a handful of fitness clubs paled in comparison to the hundreds of Rainbow franchise locations being added to the map, with a goal to reach over 1,000 systemwide. If ever there was an empire on the horizon, it sat squarely on the Brazos River at The Dwyer Group's headquarters. And the company planned to share it with the world through franchising.

The only thing I knew about franchising at that time was that all Big Macs tasted the same no matter which McDonald's you visited. What I would soon learn, however, is that replicating a business system under a brand to provide the same products or services across a growing network of peer locations didn't just end with hamburgers. Don had the brilliant idea to support a rapidly growing network of service providers doing "dirty jobs" for customers around the country, and eventually around the world, with his franchise brands. He found a pot of gold with his very first concept – Rainbow. His goal around the time I first got involved with the company was to grow that brand to 1,000 locations, and he was expanding his franchise sales team to help him get there. A sales position with this company was magic to my ears. This country boy wanted a seat at the table. There was one little wrinkle. Don's former son-in-law, Robert Tunmire, was the vice president of franchise sales, and he believed that I needed to experience the franchise concept out in the field before I could sell it. I'm not sure if the thought of doing dirty jobs was supposed to weed out the weaklings, but I was raised on dirty jobs. When the lure of selling franchises for hefty commissions was in my possible future, this kid from Axtell was up for the challenge. Keep in mind, I was also a husband and a dad who was now automotively challenged and without a real home. I wasn't in a position to negotiate. I agreed to spend six months at a Rainbow franchise to earn my stripes.

Robert got me a job with one of the Rainbow franchisees in Arlington, Texas, and I loaded up a Rainbow van with Kim, our son, Zachary, and a few belongings as we headed two hours north up the interstate. If we thought Waco was the big city after growing up in Axtell, Arlington was about to feel like Grand Central Station. Smack dab between Dallas and Fort Worth, we had an apartment that was paid for and a carpet-cleaning truck for transportation. The world was our oyster.

As luck would have it, I hit it off with the franchise owner, Mike Boedeker, right away. He was a small-town guy like me, but he had also become one of the most successful Rainbow franchisees in the rapidly expanding network. He was originally from Plainview, Texas, and had grown up as a farmer. By the looks of his franchise, he definitely knew the meaning of hard work. He had turned his Rainbow business into a million-dollar operation with almost 10 trucks on the road. I was in one of them during the hottest Texas summer, spending my days lugging heavy carpet cleaning machines in and out of the van while sprucing up people's carpets and rugs. It was nothing like the fancy vans they have today where you just pop open the back of your vehicle and roll the hose through the front door. We had to lug the whole piece of equipment with us. The machines were almost as big as me, and they were heavy. We could get stains out of carpets or, when the job required, we could dye the carpet to a desirable color and everything looked new again. With every job, we literally sucked up the money. Homes were steady income, but the big paydays, and one reason Mike did so well, came from signing up entire apartment complexes for accounts. In case I thought I had left the fitness business behind, every day was leg day on those jobs when I had to carry those machines up and down three flights of stairs at an apartment complex.

Kim, however, probably had it even worse. She hated living in Arlington. She had never been away from family and friends, and now she was in a bustling big city and felt entirely isolated at the same time. Luckily, Zachary was about one year old and a great distraction, because if Kim was meant to do anything in life, it was be a mother. Meanwhile, we were counting the days to get back to Waco when an invitation to return arrived much sooner than we expected.

Out of the blue—isn't everything in my life?—I got a phone call from a home developer in Houston. He said he was opening a mortgage company in Waco, he had been poking around at local real estate companies for talent, and somebody in town had given him my name. He wanted to know if I was interested in moving back to Waco to run this company for him. Maybe he thought I needed a little added incentive to leave the DFW area for Central Texas, so the offer came with a great salary, a new house where we could live for free, and a Volvo that I could drive. Wait, a good job that came with a house and car, too? Those were two extra things we didn't have. I was flabbergasted. I didn't even have to guess what Kim wanted me to do. While I had learned a lot about franchising by working *in* the business and not *on* the business in Arlington, I postponed my plans to sell franchises at The Dwyer Group and we hightailed it back to Waco.

We moved into a beautiful new house that even had staged furniture. Everything about our lives was picture perfect...for...

six...whole...weeks. That's when the engine went out on the Volvo and my boss had it towed. Then he told us that he couldn't fix it. Next, we found out that he had gone bankrupt. The authorities were looking for him and he had lost everything. Seemingly, so had we.

I got word that a Dallas bank was repossessing all of the new homes in the community where we lived. That's when I decided to go straight into that bank and make a deal. Well, first I had to borrow a car since I no longer had one, then I went straight to the bank. I knew we still had about 15 homes in our subdivision that had not been sold. By the look of things, the mortgage company that had planned to sell them was apparently now bankrupt. I explained to the bank that I had my real estate license and lived in that development all the way down there in Waco. I told them that I would be happy to manage the property, watch over those houses, show those houses, and do anything else they needed me to if they would let us stay. I would work for free if we could stay for free. The only alternative they had was to pay someone else to do the same thing and now have 16 empty houses to unload off their balance sheet. The bank let us live there for the next two years without paying a dime. They even covered the electric bill because they paid the energy costs on all the other unsold houses.

I returned to Waco, small victory in hand, and then made a beeline straight back to The Dwyer Group to pick up where I had left off. This time, I was not only coming back with experience after working at the Arlington franchise. My little sidestep also landed us a new house at no cost and a portfolio of homes I could manage with my eyes closed. With my old job firmly back on track, I could now make a car payment, too. All was right with the world again.

I was named a development director for Rainbow at The Dwyer Group. Finally, I was going to learn how to sell the franchise opportunity. What I went through for six months in Arlington I would now encourage others to do for their next 10 years. To explain how franchise development really works, I didn't sell franchises. I awarded the rights to operate a business under that franchise brand for a fixed amount of time, which is usually 10 years. For that privilege, a franchisee would receive business training, marketing support, access to a preferred vendor network for supplies and other services, and a protected territory in which to operate. That franchisee would also have access to a growing network of peers doing the very same thing (if they were following the system) that he or she would be doing. It's a business model that promotes the motto to be in business for yourself, but not by yourself. In order to join the club, that person would have to pay a franchise fee up front and then, depending on the terms in the Franchise Disclosure Document, pay a certain percent of sales each month in royalties back to the franchisor at headquarters. At first glance, it sounded like highway robbery. Why would anyone pay money to somebody if he, the franchisee, was going to be doing all the work?

It wasn't until I had seen a strong and proven franchise system up close that I could really experience and appreciate how the concept worked. I certainly had my front-row seat to things in Arlington. That's when I realized that franchisees invested in these kinds of opportunities so they didn't have to reinvent the wheel. The way the business functioned had already been outlined and proven by the franchisor and then replicated over and over by franchisees at locations across the map. Then, as the network grew, so did the brand's reputation and recognition. Soon enough, a Rainbow van (or 20, 50, 100 and counting) was much more impressive on the road than Lenny's Carpet Cleaning or some other mom-and-pop operator. I was an immediate believer in the business model. My next goal was to put more pins on that map, lots and lots of pins.

High-stakes sales like that took a special kind of motivation. Lucky for me, Don Dwyer learned how to do that from the very best. He was a product of SMI (Success Motivation Institute) before he founded The Dwyer Group. Yes, the same place where I waited in the lobby to pick up my wife way back when. Don had become one of the top-performing sales guys in the country there. That's also where a personal drive to be one's best had become one of the hottest commodities around. Following the playbook from SMI, Don had his sales team at The Dwyer Group create dream boards to visualize the future fruits of their labor at the company. We would create these boards and put pictures on them of incredibly expensive monetary things that we wanted for our lives. People had pictures of sports cars, Rolex watches, big houses, you name it. This was meant to inspire us and translate to franchise sales, as well as our commissions that came with them, as a means to having it all. It was the most materialistic target-setting imaginable, and I was more than eager to play along. On my dream board, I had pictures of all kinds of pricey things — my dream house, my boat, and a two-door SL450 Mercedes like the kind Bobby Ewing drove in "Dallas" on TV. Only his was red. Mine was going to be blue. I was going to possess all of those things by doing what we called "smiling and dialing."

I joke that before the invention of robocalls, there was this place called the franchise sales department at The Dwyer Group. We had mastered the stampede of franchise telemarketing, and we did our prospecting with a handy little tool called the phone book. Don had built a well-oiled machine where Robert and the franchise sales guys were offering a chance at the American Dream, a chance to be your own boss. I knew that hunger very well. I had lived it when I had my fitness club. Now, I just needed to find people who were willing to cross the finish line at Rainbow to achieve what was on the other side.

I had no idea at the time, but this was my apprenticeship into what would one day amount to awarding more than 10,000 franchises in my illustrious career. It was also my entry into one of the toughest sales pitches a person could ever make.

To this day, I tell people that if you can master the art of selling franchises, you can sell anything. It's true for any kind of franchise opportunity, and here's why. When I began awarding Rainbow deals, here's what I was really selling. I was convincing people that they needed to quit their jobs. Then they needed to take all the money they had in the bank and buy this business. Then they needed to open this business where they lived and, for all I knew, it might be the very first location for this franchise in the immediate area. They also needed to know that they weren't guaranteed a paycheck tomorrow, or the next day, or the next week. In fact, they would have to go out and market their services to win the jobs that would get that money to come in. If they could do all that, maybe they would be successful.

In layman's terms, they were going to pay my company money and then have to work really hard to get their business off the ground. It wasn't going to be easy. (Don't ever let someone tell you that you just hang out your shingle and the money comes pouring right in. I don't care what franchise opportunity somebody is selling. It will always require more than money. It will demand a lot of elbow grease, too.) That's a tough nut to crack. But as I had seen in Arlington, it was certainly a risk that people should be willing to take. I got a lot of people to take that risk. It wasn't like shooting fish in a barrel, of course. It was a lengthy sales process, and the hours spent on the phone that were required to get those deals were too long to count.

Following the sales approach that Don perfected over his career, we would come in early and leave late. But everyone took a lengthy break way longer than a lunch hour around midday. Prime time for franchise sales involved calling prospects in the morning before they went to work and then in the evenings after their families had eaten dinner. Most of these people already had a day job. Getting a good conversation started was not going to happen when they were busy answering to a boss. However, informing them that there was a way to have that title for themselves was a very powerful message. When the time was right, plenty of people were ready to take control of their future like that.

My boss led by example, coming in at 6 a.m. and staying past 10 p.m. Don was the same way. How these people ever had a family life is beyond me, but I was soon following their lead. I believe Don made it work because he had the wife and kids before he started the business. My boss, unfortunately, chalked up three divorces in the prime of his life until he got it right. As for me, I was somewhere in between. I had started a family and would add another kid to our roster – our daughter, Whitney, in 1986 – during the thick of my action at The Dwyer Group. But I also had a wife who had witnessed my definition of work ethic stretching all the way back to high school. When I wanted to focus on something, I would do whatever it took to be successful. Kim understood that and, thankfully, so did the rest of our extended family in Waco and Axtell, lending a helping hand whenever we needed one.

As I had learned on the farm, on the railroad, and at the gym, getting in first also meant moving up fast. Now at The Dwyer Group, staying at work late was expected. I did both, and my passion for franchise sales grew. Robert and Don would monitor our sales calls, help us sharpen our skills to close deals, and perfect the art of emotional selling. For example, asking potential franchisees if they wanted to work for somebody else the rest of their life always hit a nerve. Asking them if they wanted to take their family on vacation whenever they liked was a no-brainer. Being in control of one's future was a magical journey, but one that was being lived out by Rainbow franchisees all over the place. The emotional balance between earning a paycheck versus running a business was not only captivating, but also within reach. Meanwhile, my résumé to this point had delivered an uncanny ability to build strong relationships with customers, which proved invaluable when talking to these future franchisees. While a lot of people say business is business, I believe that building relationships is the single most powerful secret ingredient. And it worked extremely well in franchising, because your organization's interaction with your customer didn't end with the sale. It began with the sale and would last for years and years.

Don was my mentor during all of this and only the second millionaire I had ever known up close. Some nights, I would go up to his office where he was always working late, and we would make calls together to talk with prospects. His office was the entire top floor of this new headquarters building he had developed. You would open the door and enter this huge room, and he was still 40 feet away at this giant desk. As I walked through that door, it was like I could almost hear the angels singing. Here was this prophet of franchising to shepherd me along. It was a powerful learning experience, and it was also a great place to close deals. He was the founder and CEO, and providing access to him with some of my franchise leads was extremely attractive. It was that exchange between the corner office and that ground-floor opportunity that stuck with me forever. When I eventually occupied the C-suite in my career, I did the very same thing and still do. Being on the top rung of the ladder doesn't mean stepping on everyone to get there. You get much further when you help those along the way. I would come to understand that the best franchise models operated the same way. The franchisor doesn't succeed without the franchisee. And vice versa.

The first year I worked at The Dwyer Group, I got Rookie of the Year. I closed a lot of deals and was gifted a gold ring that top performers received. It was a really big honor. In that same time frame, I also learned what I liked about the process and what I didn't like about the process. Hitting those numbers was a huge stress. If you didn't perform, there sure as heck was somebody right behind you ready to step in and make a run at it. I also hadn't learned how to be genuinely critical of all kinds of prospects yet. I had done a ton of deals and made a ton of money, but I hadn't done enough deals to know when it was best *not* to award a franchise to someone who wouldn't make it. That's not to say that the only successful franchisees are those who can afford it. I've seen poor people become millionaires. I've also witnessed plenty of people with large bank accounts go down in flames. Back then, however, I didn't know any better, and it was all about hitting our numbers. There were the deals that would get approved so that guys could get commissions and go after those things on their dream boards. It was the '80s. Excess was in fashion. But those wins never went well. I can still remember a couple who came to Waco for Discovery Day, agreed to move forward, signed the franchise agreement, paid the franchise fee and headed for home. On the drive back, their car broke down, and now they didn't have enough money to cover the cost for a new water pump. Stories like that were incredibly revealing, especially to a country boy like me who knew what it meant to scrape up that kind of money in the first place.

Karma, however, was alive and well in franchising, and the spending and owing lessons worked both ways. Franchise sales guys who had been trained on wanting to possess big houses and fast cars on those dream boards often waved goodbye to them when the commissions slowed down and the deals dried up. I personally learned that you had to be careful what you wished for, because selling franchises just to chase money and self-indulge was not the road to happiness. The real harmony was succeeding at your job by finding the right fit for the right franchisee that offered long-term success for that owner and your brand. When you did that, the money made absolute sense.

I was nose-to-the-grindstone at this for two years when Kim's side of the family planned a huge reunion in Colorado. I told her she absolutely needed to go, but I had to stay behind and keep working. I told her I would watch the kids, and she could enjoy herself. Unknown to me, she wasn't feeling all that good, but she also hadn't seen her relatives from Arizona in a long, long time. She made the trip, and I was left to myself to work and contemplate my life. Call it a pivotal moment, but after a few days of self-reflection, I decided we all needed a change. Kim, meanwhile, spent the week with family and seven straight days throwing up. When she called in the middle of the week to check in, I told her I had something to tell her. She said, good, she had something to tell me, too. I told her to go first. She said, no, you go first. I said, "Okay, I quit my job at The Dwyer Group." She said, "Oh my gosh, I'm pregnant!"

For whatever crazy reason, I knew it would all work out. After two years of riding the wave at The Dwyer Group, I acted on an urge to put my business sense and my book smarts in proper order. I had put off college long enough and, like everything else in life, it wasn't going to be easy. After the highest of highs in franchise sales, I made the decision to quit my job, take another one for scrap money, enroll in college, and try to raise a family below the poverty line.

###

Kim said we were just young and naïve at the time. Actually, I felt like I wasn't getting any younger, and I needed to advance my education as we also kept advancing the size of our family. Right about that time, Kim's brother Danny had gone to work at a place called Waco Center for Youth. It was a housing unit for troubled kids. In return for working there, they paid for Danny to go to school and get his nursing degree. Kim's sister-in-law started working there, too. I figured, why not make it three? I applied next and got a job, starting out as a youth counselor. Like every other job I ever had, I worked hard and moved up quickly. If I needed to be there at 8 a.m., I showed up at 7:30. If I was supposed to stay until 2 p.m., I didn't leave until 3. I always did more than what was expected of me and, before I knew it, I was promoted to supervisor. I was only making $900 a month, but at least we were still in our free house.

I enrolled at McLennan Community College by Lake Waco and began working on my associate's degree in general studies. I split my time between classes and caring for these troubled kids. They were a healthy reminder that in case I thought I had it rough, they had been through things far worse. Meanwhile, Kim was at home caring for Zachary and Whitney and planning for our next child to arrive. Life seemed to be working itself out in its own twisted way when a certified letter arrived in the mail from our housing development saying, "thank you for helping us... blah, blah, blah... and you have to be out in 30 days." Our two years of free housing was over.

For a split second, we were homeless, we were broke, and we had another baby on the way. That's when somebody told Kim about a nice family in Woodway who had moved out of their home. They wanted somebody to live there, look after things, and show the property until it sold. She couldn't volunteer fast enough. Once again, we had another home for free... at least, until it was sold. Woodway was considered the wealthy suburbs of Waco. This house was humongous. It was a bi-level ranch-style house with a basement, and it was so big and dark that Kim called it "the dungeon." But it worked out well in a pinch, and that's where we lived for about the next five months. In the back of my mind, though, I knew our residential crapshoot couldn't go on forever. This was becoming a really bad habit. (Kim would later remind me that we moved 17 times in 17 years of marriage before things settled down.)

One day, we were out in Axtell visiting my mom and dad and my Aunt Julia and Uncle Travis. My uncle had just finished building this little two-bedroom house out there. It was the latest of several homes he had built on his land for rental income. The only thing this house still needed was appliances. That's when I piped up and asked him, "Hey, can we rent this from you?" He said, "Sure, let's get it finished." We did and moved right in. Our luck with free housing was over. Uncle Travis charged us a whopping $100 a month in rent. He and the rest of our family knew we were stretching to make ends meet. I also knew it was easier to be poor in Axtell than in Waco. Plus, we would have family around us to lend a helping hand. And, boy, did they ever. After we moved in, our last son, Micah, was born.

I had three kids, one wife, a low-paying job, and college classes to take care of. I had gone from having a dream board at my old job with fantasies about buying a Mercedes to not having two nickels to rub together. Between school at MCC, my job in Waco, and our home in Axtell, I was running around like a chicken with my head cut off. We all lived in a tiny two-bedroom house, at least on days I wasn't working the graveyard shift at the youth center. And somehow we managed. Other days I would work 11 p.m. to 7 a.m., went straight to my college classes until 2 p.m., back to the afternoon shift at work, and never slept an entire day, only to do the unthinkable and fall asleep at church.

Uncle Travis and Aunt Julia lived across the street from us. When she got off from her school custodial job, she would pick up Micah to help out Kim and then care for him until bedtime. They literally helped us raise that boy from the day we brought him home. Then there were countless evenings she would knock on the front door and bring over a hot dinner, and my cousin Dolores who lived behind us would knock on the back door and bring us dessert. If they knew we didn't have any food in the house, they didn't let on. But they literally saved us too many times to count.

God showed us time and again how to love your fellow man. He also reminded us how precious our time was together when he called one of us home. The one person in Axtell who couldn't be saved was Kim's dad. The pain he had been living with ever since the accident in the Arizona copper mine persisted for years. Being disabled was hard on him and hard on everyone else who wished we could make him better. He underwent back surgery, but nothing improved. It was the last straw. He kept it all to himself until he couldn't take the pain another single day. He committed suicide and threw our emotions into a tailspin. It was the lowest of lows for everyone. Kim, especially, got deeply depressed. As much as our family was there to support each other and our faith kept us all going, life was testing us in ways like never before.

To cap it all off, one morning Kim and I were having a squabble about something. We never really fought, and I certainly never let things linger. But on this particular day, I actually left the house angry and headed to work for one of many 3-p.m.-to-11-p.m. shifts at the youth center. Around midnight, as I was coming home from work and turned down our dark country road, I saw a house up in flames surrounded by fire engines. I instantly thought it was our house, and my stomach just dropped. I was paralyzed with fear, thinking that Kim and the kids were in that fire. I stepped on the gas and sped up to this inferno in the dark. As my car got closer, I could see that it was the house next door, one that was, fortunately, empty. Everyone was all right, except for me in my state of shock. That was a life-changing experience for me. From that day forward, I vowed to never leave the house angry again. I also told myself it was time to get fired up and do something different for all of us.

###

Life Lesson: *Slightly burned out but still smoking, when you get to the end of your rope, sometimes you have no choice but to keep climbing.*

5

BIG MAN ON CAMPUS

In 1991, a new health club opened up by the Baylor University campus in Waco. When Kim's cousin, my buddy Dave Hull, got a job there, I started hearing all about it. A local developer named Gordon Swanson had invested in it. Since the university didn't have anything like it for the students, he figured something called the University Fitness Club would be an instant hit. It was a high-end place and exactly what students paying high-end college tuition should have wanted. What Gordon didn't have was a salesman. Fortunately for me, Dave knew a great salesman who even had a fitness club background, so he introduced the two of us.

The opportunity could not have presented itself at a better time. I heard that Gordon was losing something like $18,000 a month at the place. He needed to sell memberships to get the ball rolling, and I was ready to make him an offer he couldn't refuse. I told him that if he hired me, I would have that place operating in the black and making money within 60 days. Gordon said, "If you can do that, I'll give you half the club." How do you like that? He actually made me an offer I couldn't refuse.

I got right to work and did what I do best. My salesman mentality went into overdrive. I not only sold memberships to Baylor students, but I also blanketed area businesses and signed up corporate accounts, too. In less than 60 days, the health club was solvent and making money for the first time ever. True to his word, Gordon gave me half of the business. I was a business owner again, my own boss, and back to running a health club.

Once I was making good money, we bought a house in Waco, packed up our things in Axtell, and moved back to town. Things at University Fitness were going so well that Gordon, a serial entrepreneur, was ready to give me full ownership of the place as he moved on to other projects around town. Gordon carried the note, I financed the second half, and now I not only owned my own gym, but I also no longer had a partner. It was the first time I was really the one and only boss of anything, and it felt good. The redneck had officially become a CEO.

My place became the social scene for students to work out and hang out. Once word got around, everyone wanted to have a membership at my place. The gym was 20,000 square feet with neon signage everywhere, the best equipment, an aerobics room that regularly filled up with 200 members in each class, and a juice bar that served smoothies. That side of campus was booming with other little businesses as well. New apartment complexes were popping up, attracting students, and my schedule was nonstop busy with work and with networking. I was so consumed with the club, in fact, that it was hard to focus on anything else. For the right occasion, however, I could make an exception. A prime example was in July 1994.

That's when I cleared my schedule to help another great businessman who was networking in town. George W. Bush had decided to run for governor. Somehow I got the honor of driving him around Waco when he was making the rounds for his campaign. We spent the day hitting all of the hot spots. He spoke to one giant crowd after another. The public's love for him was infectious. But the best part of the whole day was sitting in that car and just talking like two friends shooting the breeze. He was approachable, likable, and full of funny jokes. I had a pretty strong gut instinct I would be calling him Gov. Bush real soon. Who could have guessed I was driving around a future U.S. president, too? He was the nicest guy and a hard worker. In fact, his schedule was so busy gearing up for the election that he gave me his tickets to the next Texas Rangers baseball game in Arlington. As the team's owner, he had the best seats in the entire ballpark. I gladly accepted his tickets for what turned out to be one of the best gifts I've ever received. On July 28, 1994, I watched Kenny Rogers of the Texas Rangers pitch only the 14th perfect game in Major League Baseball history, beating the California Angels 4-0. I'm sure our future Texas governor was sad to miss the historic event, but his generosity toward me made a lifelong impression. To this very day, I am always looking to go that extra step to take care of those around me. It was the same in my business, too.

If I had learned anything this far in my career, it was to never rest on my laurels. My work ethic never allowed me to coast. As business at University Fitness evolved, I had a keen focus to always keep the club in tip-top shape. What I had witnessed at my first club, when my dad wanted to cut costs and raise prices, was the opposite of my mindset this time around. I constantly wanted to invest in the business that was paying strong returns.

I kept an eye on the latest and greatest equipment for my space, and I would attend industry trade shows to stay focused on where things were headed. Over the years, I had been ordering high-end fitness equipment from Powercise, where fellow Texan Gary Heavin was my sales contact. It was the most advanced equipment on the market at the time with features that actually spoke to you. We had never met in person, but I had dealt with Gary a number of times. When I placed my orders, the equipment always arrived as promised. He worked on commission, and his customer service showed.

I was attending the International Health, Racquet and Sportsclub Association (IHRSA) trade show in California when I took a break between sessions on an outside bench. A gentleman sat down next to me to do the same, and we struck up a conversation. Being a friendly country boy, I always talked to strangers. He asked me my name, and I said, "Gary." He smiled and said, "Oh, my name is Gary, too. Gary Heavin." I said, "Hey, I buy equipment from you." Here were two boys from Texas who went all the way to California to meet each other. We chatted about fitness, about equipment, about his career journey, and about mine. I shared my highs and lows, how I was on my second health club, how the first one went south, and about my time in franchise development at The Dwyer Group. Gary had his own ups and downs as well, starting a string of gyms in Texas called Women's World of Fitness before going bust and selling fitness equipment for a living. Neither one of us had waltzed into success. We both had our fair share of sweaty days and hard work long before we got into fitness. He had been a roughneck on oil rigs, a longshoreman, a waiter, and a truck driver. His dream of becoming a doctor fizzled out when the money to cover school did, too. I had been a railroad man, worked with juvenile delinquents, and been homeless and poor more than once. Our strongest connection, however, was that we both had an incredible passion for the fitness business, even though we both had lost it all before. Two Garys became instant friends on that bench that day. I was as much about building relationships as I was about building a business, so I knew we would stay in touch.

Speaking of relationships and staying in touch, my former employer resurfaced one day while I was running my club. I received a subpoena to appear in court. I was expected to testify in Fort Worth in a case between the home office and a certain Rainbow franchisee from Arlington. The guy I shadowed when I started working at Rainbow had decided to exit the system and go out on his own. In the world of franchising, you can't just break a franchise agreement and go renegade. If a franchisee isn't happy with the business but loves the industry, he or she needs to finish out the agreement and simply not renew the contract. I didn't know the details, but this wasn't my fight. I had worked with this franchisee up close, and I had worked for corporate, too. The attorney for the Arlington franchisee subpoenaed me, so somewhere along the line my testimony was expected to help his case. Either way, I had no problem going to court and sharing anything I knew to be correct and true. Don, however, wanted to shut this guy down.

I drove to Fort Worth, arrived at court, and sat down to answer questions. Don and Robert were there with their legal team. The former Rainbow franchisee was there with his attorney. And then there was me. The defending attorney asked me, "Did you sell franchises?" I said, yes. Then he started asking me about the date that documents got signed when franchises were sold. The evidence showed that dates on multiple franchise agreements had been backdated. I did remember that Don traveled a lot and needed time to look at them and sign them. But in fact, this shortened the overall window for the franchisee. It meant The Dwyer Group was beating the clock on the Franchise Disclosure Document, which, by federal law, mandated that a prospective franchisee could not sign the franchise agreement or pay the franchise fee until he or she had possessed the FDD for 14 full calendar days. The judge heard all that he needed to hear and said, "Case dismissed." The former Rainbow franchisee won the judgment, and I had just testified against my former employer. I had painted a negative picture for this millionaire and mentor, who probably would have paid a handsome penny to win this case. I was sure I burned a bridge, but I was also sure that I told the truth to the extent that I knew it. I wasn't trying to make everyone happy; I was trying to do what was right. If there was one thing I liked about Don Dwyer, it was that he didn't tolerate a weasel. He could appreciate people who were honest.

As I was leaving court, Robert walked up to me and asked if I wanted to come back and work for them. He even offered me a ride back in their plane to talk about it. This was just after I had testified against them. I kindly passed on the offer, but I secretly admired that Don could appreciate my integrity through the whole process. He was a man who fought for what he believed in, and he also could be ruthless when he needed to be. But he knew this wasn't my axe to grind. That outcome and how he reacted always stuck with me. Still, we both had our own businesses to run. Don was busy building a franchise empire, and I was happy at my gym. That would be the last time I saw Don Dwyer.

In 1994, Don suffered a massive stroke and died at the age of 60. He had realized a lifelong dream the year before when he took The Dwyer Group public on the NASDAQ, trading under the symbol DWYR. After his untimely death, Robert stepped into the lead role as CEO for a while. Meanwhile, I watched from a distance down the road at my fitness club. Things hardly seemed as shaky where I was the boss. By comparison, I was a small-business owner who was sure that I had a firm hold on the reins of my operation. It would soon come falling down like a house of cards.

Thanks to the savings and loan crisis, banks were having a horrible time and closing left and right. When the bubble burst, our shopping center went into foreclosure, and the government took over. Since University Fitness was the one big tenant keeping this property alive, we were able to renegotiate the lease from $11,000 to $4,000 a month. Being a strong anchor tenant, the government really worked with me. The health club was an asset that could keep the commercial space safe, functional and, best of all, occupied. Eventually, however, the government sold the shopping center at auction where a new landlord purchased it for pennies on the dollar. The minute he owned it, he wanted to raise my rent from $4,000 to $8,000 a month. Gordon flew me up to Lewisville, a Dallas suburb, in his plane so we could meet with the new landlord. Gordon explained that if he jacked up the rent, he would put me out of business, the shopping center would become a ghost town, and everyone else would leave. None of that changed my new landlord's mind. My uphill battle had arrived. It came with another competitor, too.

There was only so much success that could happen in the shadow of a major Division 1-A university before the institution saw an opportunity. As students worked on their health and fitness at my gym, my bottom line continued to look okay until the other shoe dropped and the bubble decided to burst. After several years of financial security for the Findley household and University Fitness, perhaps the end was near. A major initiative was being discussed by Baylor's administration to bump up campus life, support a lot more than time spent in class, and engage students to stick around campus rather than run off to have fun.

Kim's cousin Dave, the same person who had led me to University Fitness Center, also had a job on the Baylor campus. That's where he heard a rumor that the university was going to build a new fitness center with state-of-the art amenities. In case I thought I had a nice gym serving my members, I could only imagine what Baylor would build for more than 10,000 students.

While Baylor students previously had access to Russell Gymnasium with a small weight room on campus, there was no dedicated, full-fledged club. That was all about to change. The administration approved the development of a new Baylor Fitness Center in the Goebel building. It would offer 7,000 square feet of space with 70 pieces of equipment, including stationary bikes, Stairmasters, free weights, and more. The center would open at 6:30 a.m., would close from 8 a.m. to 3 p.m. each day for physical education classes in the shared space, and reopen in the evening. They would not have personal trainers or formal classes, but everyone was free to do what they wanted. Worst of all for me, the new Baylor Fitness Center would be open to all students, faculty, and staff with a valid Baylor ID. Thanks to a $50 student activity fee each semester, the university destroyed my monthly membership fee and had more than enough money to offer something attractive on campus instead.

I was about to come face to face with a tough business lesson: location, location, location. While a good health club right next to campus had been providing me with a great living, a health club on campus that was practically free was about to put me out of a job. I had been a mom-and-pop operation with a captive audience for years but the 800-pound gorilla next door could outspend me with his eyes closed. In the blink of an eye, my gym's reputation went from big man on campus to little guy in no man's land. I was lost.

I tried convincing myself that a stronger fitness brand might help me be competitive. At the eleventh hour when I should have thrown in the towel, I dug in my heels, paid a $5,000 licensing fee, and rebranded my space as Powerhouse Gym. I went into deeper debt to keep the doors open and then waited to live through the outcome of my decisions. When Baylor opened the doors to its new fitness center in September 1994, my gym became a ghost town overnight. We closed one week later.

The writing was on the wall. My business had gone bust. I knew it, and so did all of my friends and family. As my lease for the space was coming up, my landlord got aggressive about negotiating the renewal. There was absolutely nothing to renew as far as I was concerned. I was sure he would just change the locks and hold my equipment hostage inside if I didn't act quickly. That's when I made the decision to close our doors for good. We informed our few remaining loyal members, watched them file out as the sun went down on our last day, locked the front doors behind them, and quietly opened the back doors. Trucks and trailers were waiting to load all of the equipment and take it to storage. Unlike years before, when I watched Allen Stanford file bankruptcy and walk away, I planned to sell all of my assets, get every penny I could, and pay every last creditor I owed no matter how long it took.

Gordon — the same guy who put me up in that business, gave me half-ownership, and then gave me the whole thing on a note — was the first one there that night with his trucks and his team. He knew at that point that he was going to lose thousands of dollars. I walked up to him in the middle of the night as the place was being emptied, and I said, "If it takes everything I've got, I will never live my life without paying you back." He looked right at me and said, "You know what, Gary? You don't owe me a dime. You did everything you could, and you did great things for this club while it lasted." He did me an incredible favor by forgiving that debt. Thankfully, I can say now that Gordon would make back that money tenfold from me and others.

If he had a crystal ball and could see the future, I'm sure he would have never built the gym in the first place, let alone given it to me, only to see me go bankrupt. Regardless of that outcome, I will always consider him a lifelong friend for showing me that I could be the boss again. I was just a victim of unforeseen circumstances: the economy's impact on the banking system and Baylor's dedicated service to its student body. My business bit the dust, thanks to unrealistic rent and a university that saw me catering to students and decided to do it even better. I never lost my dignity. We had a good run for seven years, but I held on too long. After hitching my wagon to a college crowd that came in full force, it was eventually thanks to their school that I was also personally bankrupt at the end.

We worked all night long and cleared out the place. When we were done, I drove home and went straight to bed. I wasn't sure what tomorrow would bring. Heck, it was already tomorrow. But the anxiety of it all was finally over. I slept hard and I slept long. For once, I didn't need to be up early to go to work. Oddly enough, Kim reacted the same way. She had known the gym was closing and she knew we were clearing out the space that night, too. Still, she slept like a rock just like me. She said she was at peace with it all because she knew it would be all right. Lo and behold, it was.

The next morning at 10 o'clock, our phone rang. It was Robert, now the CEO at The Dwyer Group. He said, "I heard you just closed your club down, and I want you to know that you have a job here if you want it."

If there's anything that perks up your ears after you've just gone bankrupt, it's a steady job. Just like that, I was back in the game. I went back to The Dwyer Group eight years after I had worked there the first time. I was eight years wiser as well. After closing the club, I was forced to file bankruptcy due to the business debt. Failing in business for the very first time on my own dime provided a newfound critical eye on when and how to award franchises, too. I was ready to make a difference for those who were right for the opportunity.

I returned as a vice president of franchise sales for Rainbow in 1995, a brand I knew well but at an office that looked a whole lot different. I was immersed in a brand-new world at headquarters. While I had been away running my gym, The Dwyer Group had added several other service brands to the roster, strengthening its position as a major player in franchising. The place was a growing enterprise of multiple franchise opportunities fueled by a franchise development team and a goal to sell, sell, sell. So, in some ways, as much as the company had changed and grown, the culture in franchise sales was immediately familiar. There was no debate that the organization was doing well. After losing my health club, I was ready to start doing well again, too. It even crossed my mind that this could be where I finished out my career. I stayed in my lane and got busy. I got busy selling, but I also got busy learning.

If I thought I knew about franchising from my first stint at The Dwyer Group, I greatly enhanced my skills when I returned. I suddenly had the inside track on how a growth vehicle not only worked for one brand, but many. My first time around, I had been awarding franchise opportunities for an established network, the Rainbow concept that launched the organization. Now I could see how the same approach worked to build other brands from the ground up or through acquisitions of like-minded franchise networks. Suddenly, the teachable moments went above and beyond franchise development.

My second turn at The Dwyer Group was not just about working leads and closing deals. I also paid very close attention to what was needed after the ink dried. I studied how the headquarters staff helped franchisees open successfully, addressed and solved local needs from the network, provided advanced training, and approved when someone was ready to be a multi-unit operator (of more than one franchise location). It was no longer just about sales. My view was all about the big picture. If I already understood how to grow one brand, this time I saw sister brands make the same journey. I was motivated to learn that the franchise business model was a scalable approach for one, two, three, four, and more growing networks under one parent company. The opportunities were endless and The Dwyer Group was certainly on to something. By 1995, all of their service franchise brands addressed the same potential customer base across Rainbow, Mr. Rooter Plumbing, Aire Serv Heating & Air Conditioning, and Mr. Electric. In a world where many people are not do-it-yourselfers, consumers needed these services when they wanted a true expert. The Dwyer Group also ran two brands called General Business Services and EKW, which offered tax, payroll, and business counseling services to their franchisees and to all types of small-business owners. While business services weren't a natural fit and those brands would later be sold off, the dirty jobs across the service trades were an absolute gold mine. I had become a student in the school of franchising when I returned to The Dwyer Group, and it provided me with a lifelong lesson that I carry to this day. With the right concept, franchising could do wonders. In fact, it could propel all kinds of solid business ideas into gigantic success stories.

That was just my observation from being on the inside, of course.

It's not like I had another concept to go test this out. Plus, I was busy with my day job of growing Rainbow. It was only a theory. Then one day my phone rang.

My buddy Gary Heavin from my gym days called. We had stayed in touch ever since we first met back at the IHRSA show in California. He was an entrepreneur at heart like me. He was also a hard worker like me. Ahem, he had also been a failure in business...again, like me. We could always find plenty of things to talk about to fill a phone call. He never disappointed, and this time was certainly no different.

Gary knew that my second club had gone under. He also knew I had gone back to work for The Dwyer Group in franchise sales. Call it fate, but both of us actually had changed jobs since we first met. The guy who used to sell me gym equipment now wanted my advice on selling franchises. Wait, what? He had opened a small business down in the Valley, grown it to a couple of locations in South Texas, and it was doing rather well. It was doing so well, in fact, that he thought it was the kind of business that would make a good franchise.

He had my interest.

Life Lesson: No cattle means you have no fences. Live your life like there are no boundaries to the success you have.

6

BACK IN THE SADDLE

Gary Heavin had been living down in Harlingen, Texas, near the Mexico border, when the entrepreneurial bug struck again. He had previously grown a women-only fitness concept with his brother in the Houston area years before. They expanded to 14 locations and stretched the build-out to bigger retail spaces and higher rents in the process. However, the theory that everything is bigger in Texas worked only for so long.

His business ended, his marriage ended, and he went flat broke—to the point that he also served time in jail for failure to pay child support. If there was ever someone who had been down on his luck, it was Gary back then. That's right about when he gave in to a higher power. He found his faith, rededicated himself to Christ, and also turned his life around. He landed on his feet, got into fitness equipment sales, and later got remarried. Gary had a new wife, Diane, and a new outlook on a business idea with some serious muscle.

In 1992, Gary and Diane opened a little fitness center called Curves for Women in Harlingen. As Gary discovered, smaller was better this time around, with a very important bonus: It looked profitable.

The physical space of the business was tiny by comparison for the fitness industry, but it was perfect for available retail space with low monthly rent. Like before, this business only catered to women. The secret was a 30-minute circuit where women worked out across a fixed number of fitness machines configured in a circle. Start to finish, the customer could come in at any time, hop on the circuit, and be done and on her way in half an hour. It was an instant hit in Harlingen. Before Gary got too excited, he opened two other locations in McAllen and Brownsville over the next two years to prove (or disprove) his luck with the first. They both opened well, were equally successful, and sustained a great crowd of members for months and months. His highest hopes had been confirmed. He perfected the operations side and Diane, who had a background in advertising, finessed the marketing.

By now, Gary figured he could keep right on growing as fast as his limited capital would allow. But his past bankruptcy was hardly a distant memory. Maybe, just maybe, he could invite others onto his bandwagon to really get things moving. He had already duplicated the concept more than once. Why couldn't others do the same?

That's about the time my phone rang.

He had a winner on his hands. That much he knew. He had opened three locations in four years that were all doing well. Now he wanted to expand it faster. He wanted to do it under the radar before a competitor tried to copy the idea. He also wanted to know from me if he could do it by franchising the concept.

He asked me what I could do to help. To begin with, he needed to know what a franchise opportunity looked like on paper. The single, most important thing a prospective franchisee would need to see is the Franchise Disclosure Document (FDD). That would outline the investment, the requirements, the historical background on the company and, most importantly, keep Uncle Sam happy. The FDD was, after all, required by law. Nobody could award a franchise until the federal government said so. And, after that, the FDD had to be filed individually with each state as well.

To explain what a tried-and-true franchise opportunity looked like in legal terms, I sent him an FDD from Rainbow at The Dwyer Group. Nothing about a carpet cleaning and dyeing company was similar to a fitness club, but that didn't matter. The sections of an FDD were the same whether your franchise made donuts, painted houses, booked vacations, changed the oil in your car or filed your taxes. It carried the standard language that any reputable franchisor had to disclose. It also showed the good, the bad, and the ugly. A franchisor had to share lawsuits filed against the company or legal troubles among its leaders. It had to provide a whole list of franchisees in the system with their contact information. This is done so an interested prospect could call and find out how happy or unhappy people were with the investment. It had to disclose franchisees who had closed, too, so prospects doing their due diligence could reach out to ask if they failed, lost all their money, or just decided not to renew an agreement and why. For a brand-spanking-new opportunity, these sections remained empty until the right guinea pigs came along and decided to be first.

The FDD would also list the financial requirements necessary to run the business and the ongoing royalties to be paid to the franchisor in return. It would explain what a franchisee must comply with in order to do business. For example, a McDonald's franchisee could never go rogue and start serving pizza. It wasn't in the FDD. The franchisor could then terminate the agreement for non-compliance. It was a complicated document required by the federal government and it supported a booming cottage industry of franchise attorneys who specialized in creating them. I was a country boy who looked at these all day long. These legal contracts had been intimidating to me at first. Now they were second nature to me and offered full transparency to all parties involved.

Gary looked over the example I provided and was back on the phone with me in no time. He needed more than just an FDD document as his guide. He needed someone to actually sell his opportunity. He had developed the business model, and now he wanted me to jump in with him and grow the thing.

I couldn't lie. It sure sounded exciting. But he and I were broker than broke. On top of that, I wasn't blind to the fact that I had followed my dreams before and, regardless of the long hours and hard work, I had put my family in the poorhouse one too many times. Kim had always supported my decisions, but the adversity we had gone through was hard to overlook. I was one cowboy who couldn't keep pressing my luck with my bride. I had three kids to raise, a fresh bankruptcy to my name, and debts to pay. How could I honestly convince her that I should leave a growing international franchise organization with locations around the world and a solid paycheck under my belt to go and test something out on a hunch down at the border? I had only been back at Rainbow for eight months.

If there was one man who understood that kind of career rollercoaster, it was Gary Heavin. He didn't want me to make a hasty decision. He told me that Kim and I should both drive down, see things for ourselves, and then I could decide. It was a no-harm-no-foul kind of offer. I could bring Kim along, get a road trip out of it, and walk away without a second thought if we weren't completely sold.

To be honest, that seemed innocent enough. In the back of my mind, however, I could see a hardheaded bull rider who kept getting bucked off, stomped on, and broken—and dang if he didn't keep getting on another bull. What if fitness clubs were my bucking bull? I still had raw memories from the failures of my first club with my father and my second club on my own. Surrendering to those losses was difficult. They also gave me a big dose of humility. I sure as heck didn't want to walk into failure for a third time. Yet, something about this was different. The idea of franchising this business added an undeniable charm to it all. I decided to tell Kim about the invitation and see what she thought. Ironically, Kim never worried about anything in good times or bad. She was sure that the good Lord would always provide and, despite my professional ups and downs, He certainly did. But I was stunned when she agreed to go with me and check out Curves. Following the past entrepreneurial hurdles I had brought to our marriage, she made me promise that I was done for good when I returned to The Dwyer Group. I wholeheartedly agreed. How could I not? Yet, there we went, heading down the interstate to see this tiny little place called Curves. For some completely illogical reason, we both had an open mind, and what we found was a wide open door to our future.

###

When we arrived to see Gary and Diane, we all hit it off. Kim could tell that they were honest-to-goodness hard-working people, strong Christians like us, and very eager to show us the business. All friendliness aside, they wanted a frank opinion on where this could go. We got the official tour of Curves in mere minutes. Yep, that's how small the place was. It was also the key ingredient to the company's success. The first location was 1,500 square feet and a shining beacon, if there ever was one, for an anti-club. There were no treadmills, no saunas, no locker rooms, no showers, no aerobics classrooms, no free weights and no daycare rooms. Instead, there were eight hydraulic resistance machines, perfect for the square footage, in a round configuration. Women paid a monthly membership, arrived anytime the doors were open, and went through each station in the circuit for a complete, full-body workout in 30 minutes. It was so easy that it was ingenious. The standard workout could burn up to 500 calories in a single visit. Gary and Diane were convinced they were onto something. I was convinced they were, too.

Kim and I left there and definitely wanted to give it a run. I told Gary up front that I was not relocating my family. He said that was fine. I could work from my house in Waco, and he would work from his house in Harlingen. I would be the vice president and handle franchise development, and he would be the founder and CEO and handle operations and the manufacturing of the fitness equipment for every franchise we opened. We would see if this thing really had legs. Before I even got back in the car to head to Waco, I knew I was about to fly the coop and leave Rainbow and The Dwyer Group for a second time. Instead of representing a brand that had reached 1,000 franchise locations in 10 years, I was going to willingly represent a brand that had zero franchise locations and what I considered a glimmer of hope. It was either the craziest thing I would ever do or I was about to start the adventure of a lifetime.

I had walked into existing fitness clubs before to eventually take them over and be my own boss. But, as I had seen from my days at Rainbow, each time I was an independent owner-operator who lacked the business training, marketing support, peer collaboration, and purchasing power that an entire franchise network could offer. I lacked a serious brand with any real clout beyond my four walls and my customers. I also knew firsthand that those customers could easily be lured elsewhere. Now I was going to launch a franchise from the ground up and let everyone be the boss of their own fitness business. Together, who knows what we could accomplish? We might possibly become a household name. Something about it sounded incredibly fun. It would also be insanely hard. Lucky for me, having fun and working hard were two things I did very well.

In January 1996, I gave my notice at work, crossed my fingers, and did some serious praying to the man above that I had made the right decision. I was 35 years old and trying to be a responsible adult. Meanwhile, I surrendered completely to the fitness industry that I loved and dove headfirst into my strongest growing talent: franchise sales. The next few weeks, months, and years were about to become a whirlwind.

How we got things off the ground was a total mystery to me. First, we had this FDD on this brand-new company. It said the only two people at the company were these two guys named Gary and they both had bankruptcies. As ridiculous as it sounded, franchise prospects would read this and actually have to tell themselves, "This guy went bankrupt, and this guy went bankrupt, and now we're going to buy a business from them."

To help win over that sale, our only marketing materials consisted of a self-designed, three-page brochure that Gary had put together. The front and back were black with a pink Curves for Women logo. The inside pages had a few photos of a club and equipment. I don't think it even had investment details. Nevertheless, Gary was extremely proud of this marketing brochure. He had one of these binding machines at his house, so we would print these pages, bind them up, and I would take them in quantities of 20 at a time as some kind of homerun sales tool. Knowing what other franchisors had to show potential investors, this was the worst piece of collateral I could give somebody and expect them to want to buy a business. Pardon my poor country etiquette, but this was about as half-assed as we could get.

That made what happened next all the more surreal.

If I could pat myself on the back for anything at all on day one, it was my ability to sell franchises with that FDD and that brochure as my only tools. There was no way we should have won deals right out of the gate, but we did.

My plan of attack to start rounding up leads was to target small cities similar to Harlingen's size where the brand had already succeeded. I placed advertisements in local newspapers in towns across Texas, Colorado, Oklahoma, and Arkansas. The ads announced that a new franchise was coming to town and it was the hottest fitness center for women only. I listed my contact information to meet and learn more. Then I made appointments, hopped in the car, drove to those towns, and met with prospects. I never got more than two appointments off of a single ad but, lucky for me, that's all this cowboy needed. Like they say in Texas, "one riot, one Ranger." I never went to a town where I didn't close a deal. No matter what, when I met with someone, I sold a franchise. I hit the next town, met with someone else, and sold another franchise. Then on the drive back, I hit another town, met with someone else, and sold another franchise. I was completely in the zone. God had to be smiling down on me. That was the only explanation to make any sense of it all. I was scoring a perfect batting average for a business that nobody had ever seen or heard about.

On the other hand, who could blame them? I was a great salesman but, quite honestly, the business Gary and Diane had created was also hotter than hot. It was attractive because it was so incredibly simple to execute. A standard Curves franchise had very few moving parts. We designed the offer so you could literally buy a franchise on a credit card. The franchise fee was only $19,900, and that included all of the fitness equipment. All in, franchisees could be up and running for less than $30,000. In other words, it cost less to open and own your own business than it did to buy a new car.

We also found a real estate guru, John McCord, who later became a great friend. John could go into these small towns and locate the perfect real estate for as little as $200 per month on the lease. The build-out was minimal. Paint, signage, and the delivery of equipment had someone up and running in no time. It was only a matter of weeks between the time the ink was dry on the franchise agreement and opening day. Plus, the operating expenses were so low that the break-even point for franchisees was super quick after a membership drive. The ace in the hole, the thing that sealed the deal, was the women-only membership. There was nothing like it on the market. Hands down, women loved the idea of working out when it fit their schedules and being done in 30 minutes. They could do it with their girlfriends. It became like a club. The novelty of it and the idea that they would not be intimidated by sweaty men who worked out at other gyms was instantly attractive. So was the idea of owning one.

As I started selling, I met with all kinds of people. Husbands often financed these franchises for wives to run. Women invested in Curves as a second career. People came out of retirement to do something fun with their time. Parents bought franchises to set their children up in business. You name it, the fit was right. In those early days, I only awarded one franchise at a time, but the satisfaction was immediate. Most importantly, women felt empowered as business owners, and their customers (also women) felt healthier as fitness members. We were giving a voice to a segment of the population who hadn't received this kind of unconditional attention before. Straight out of the gate, Curves was on a roll. I was busier than I ever thought possible.

Kim and I put a fax machine in our bedroom, and the thing went off at all hours of the day and night. These were the franchise leads who had called off of the newspaper ads wanting to set up an appointment with me when I came to town. For the first hour of every day, it was like unraveling the Dead Sea Scrolls. Kim and

I would get our scissors—she would get on one end and I would get on the other. We would stretch out this unending sheet of fax paper and begin cutting it into individual 8 ½-by-11 pages so I could see where all of my prospects lived. Those markets then determined which cities I would hit in what order. This was our highly sophisticated franchise development headquarters at work.

I could tell immediately that I was about to have a busy life on the road. That's when we found a way to mix business with pleasure. If I was going to spend so much time behind the wheel trying to win these deals, then why not bring the family along and make it a vacation? The first geography we wanted to target was Colorado. It was a completely selfish way to grow the brand in a state we loved. Kim and the kids packed the car and we made the most out of our unknown future. Franchise development co-mingled with camping and sightseeing. Then, without any explanation at all, I kept making sales on a completely unknown franchise opportunity, and this became our new normal. Summer break turned into Curves expansion. As Curves got off the ground, I also made the most out of showing more of our great country to our kids at each turn. Even during the school year, for every new state I ventured into, I would pick a child and bring them along. I took Whitney to Oklahoma, Micah to Arkansas, and Zachary to New Mexico. I would meet with a franchise prospect at a local restaurant, and there was my child, reading a book or coloring right next to us.

To say that my family grew up alongside the Curves business was figuratively and literally true. I took the kids on so many road trips, in fact, that Kim opened a letter from the school district one day telling us that they were missing too much school. In spite of making good grades (our prerequisite for tagging along), they still had to meet attendance requirements. That was fair enough. If I expected franchisees to comply with the FDD rules at Curves, I guess our kids could comply with the attendance rules at school. That never slowed down my long and now somewhat more lonely travel, of course. I had become a serious road warrior, and my duties didn't end with franchise sales, either.

Curves was a full-fledged startup, and I had to wear many, many hats. I was the franchise sales guy, the equipment deliveryman, the grand-opening helper, and the membership drive support team. In the early days, I would make a swing across a few towns, sell a few franchises, drive back to Waco to see the family, and get back in the car and drive six-and-a-half hours to Harlingen. That's where a trailer full of fitness equipment was ready to be loaded, and then I would drive it to whichever Curves location was next in line to open. I would assemble the equipment in that new location and then help with the grand-opening festivities. I would even sign up new members.

Ladies in all of these small towns found me a little peculiar. Who was the redneck at the door signing them up at a gym that only allowed women? Our marketing message for the business was "no men, no men, no men." Then women came to a grand opening and there I was, this man, selling them their membership. My country boy charm earned their forgiveness. They paid to join Curves, business got off to a great start, and I was back on the road to do it all over again.

Handling these one at a time was doable at the start, and Gary and I saw things take shape very quickly. He appreciated what I brought to the company, and he paid me very well from the minute the business got going. Then, one night, we were sitting on the floor of his garage assembling fitness equipment for a delivery when he made me the deal of the century. Gary said, "I don't want partners. I've never wanted partners." (That was after he had a partner who sued him.) So he said, "I'll make you a deal. You'll have a salary, and I will give you 10 percent of the profits of the company every year. And if we sell or you decide to leave, I'll give you 10 percent of the value of the company." Sure, why not? It sounded pretty good to me. We made it official and shook on it. Neither one of us knew, but sitting on the floor of that garage, I had just made the most lucrative business agreement of my life with nothing more than a handshake.

Then came a wave of grand openings. Before too long, I was down in Harlingen on a regular basis to haul equipment to new locations. Now, if there was one thing I thought we would invest in at an early stage, it was our transportation for all of this equipment. But never mind that doggone silly thinking. Gary figured we had all that we needed to get the job done. Thus, began my love-hate relationship with our affectionate trailer. I was a redneck who knew my way around a trailer, but Gary's flatbed trailer was more like a sick horse that needed to be shot. Gary and I would strap down a new supply of fitness equipment on this open-air, rag-tag thing, and I counted my lucky stars if I didn't get a flat tire before I got to my destination. Gary also handed me a little red toolbox for every drive. I couldn't deliver equipment without it. The first time he gave it to me, I said, "What's that?" He said, "These are all of the things that you'll need." Inside was a screwdriver, a special cleaner, and a can of white spray paint. That's how beat-up this brand-new equipment got on that raggedy trailer. Every time I was about to reach a new location, first I had to stop, clean off the bugs and dirt that had splattered all over the equipment from the ride, and spray paint on all of the new scratches from banging around on the open road.

Still, I figured a little franchise growth and a little cash would change all that, right? When we hit our stride, we had more openings, more equipment orders, and more deliveries to make. Now I had to haul fitness equipment to multiple locations in one trip. It was obvious that ol' trailer wasn't going to work any longer. Money was coming in, too. For crying out loud, Gary could go down the street and buy a bigger trailer by now. Sure enough, that's when he said he had a new trailer for me.

The next time I arrived, I found out my so-called new trailer was really the old trailer with another five feet added onto the back. Gary had the guy who manufactured our fitness equipment do it. I can't explain the lousy redneck physics of just making an old trailer longer to carry more equipment and more weight on the same wobbly tires. Nonetheless, there I went, pulling twice the load out on the highway and holding my breath on any kind of pavement with a steep incline.

A little more time passed, and more sales meant more openings. Now the equipment orders were really piling up. I showed up one day in Harlingen to find out Gary had added a second story to our trailer. He had also found a way to get three pieces of equipment in the back of the Suburban pulling it all. Were we growing a franchise or running a carnival? One look at that contraption and it was a little hard to tell. How I was never stopped by the cops on those runs was astounding. I was a moving violation and a danger to every other car on the road. The adventures didn't stop there.

We eventually graduated from our trailer to multiple 6-by-12 U-Haul trailers. Hallelujah, we finally had covered transportation. That saved me a little less cleaning and spray painting on equipment runs. But even the U-Hauls soon got abused. Business started getting so big so fast that we soon resorted to strapping extra equipment on the roof of the U-Hauls in addition to the full load inside. As ludicrous as some of our decisions were, we did anything and everything necessary to make things work. And I never missed a delivery. That's how committed we were to building our network, supporting our franchisees, and starting off strong. Nothing could hold me down... even on one fateful trip when all I wanted to do was keep something down.

One day, I had to make a run to a grand opening in Canyon City, Colorado. I was driving up on a Sunday, leaving in the morning from Harlingen, arriving in Colorado Sunday night, and setting up equipment to be ready to open the first thing on Monday. I woke up that Sunday morning with the worst stomach flu of my life. I was throwing up every 10 minutes. I couldn't keep anything down. Meanwhile, Gary was off somewhere else, so it was up to me to make the equipment run, or Canyon City would have the worst Curves grand opening imaginable. I had the equipment already loaded, so there was no time to waste. We couldn't open a fitness gym without a lick of equipment on the floor. I had to hit the road. The entire drive was nothing but a series of stops. I would drive for a while, get out, throw up, and get back in the truck and keep going. I would make it a few more miles and repeat it all over again. This went on forever. At one point, I was so exhausted, I couldn't make it a minute longer. I got a hotel room, went inside, laid down, and slept for about four hours. I woke up, got back behind the wheel, and kept on trucking. Somehow I made it to the Canyon City location before sunrise that Monday. I pulled up into a dark and empty parking lot with barely enough energy to unload the equipment onto the pavement in front of the club. Then I sat down on one of the pieces of equipment and fell sound asleep sitting up. The only thing that woke me was this intense bright light that hit me right in the face as the sun crept up over the horizon at sunrise. I squinted into the sun, looked at my watch, saw that it was 6:30 in the morning, and watched a car pull up right beside me. It was the franchisee.

Operating hours for Curves locations were 8 a.m. to noon, followed by a four-hour break when the team was out marketing, and back again from 4 p.m. until closing time. We had only 90 minutes to get everything sitting in the parking lot through those doors and ready for this club's official grand opening. We got the doors unlocked, hustled as best we could and were finished just in time when people arrived at 8 a.m. for the festivities. The gym closed at noon. I went to a hotel, got some more rest, and thankfully was no longer sick. I returned to the club at 4 p.m. when it reopened and finished out the day. It was the closest call I ever had for a Curves grand opening and, as far as my franchisee was concerned, it was a smashing success. The franchisee could close up, claim victory, head home, and relax until tomorrow. For me, it was time to get back on the road and drive all the way back to South Texas.

Wrangling all those leads, herding all that equipment, and turning hard work and sweat into new locations and a growing reputation was every bit as exhausting as it was rewarding. For the first time in my life, I was becoming successful beyond my dreams. And I loved every bit of it.

To hear the way my kids tell it, things were just better. In the coming years, we drove better cars, we lived in better houses, and we had a better life. But making money never changed their dad. I had a rock-solid conviction about the value of hard work, and they would know it as well. From the day we launched Curves, my bank account began to transform beyond imagination. My principles, in the meantime, remained exactly the same. Thank goodness I was just a country boy with strong faith, a big dose of small-town gumption, and a burning desire to succeed. I credit those things for making it all possible.

###

Life Lesson: *Broke as a field mouse. The myth that you must have money to make money is exactly that, a myth. Don't settle for the status quo. Changing my status quo changed my life.*

7

RIDE OF A LIFETIME

The best memories I made while growing the Curves network were the wild and crazy things we did and learned along the way. First and foremost, dreaming about making money and actually making money were two entirely different things. For dang sure, we didn't comprehend how fast the system would grow. We were so busy making things happen that the money wasn't even our focus. I can remember we started receiving these checks for franchise fees, and one day Gary left my house with a FedEx envelope containing three or four of these checks inside. We had reached maybe 20 deals so far, and now he had thousands and thousands of dollars in his hands. You might think he would be obsessed with getting it straight to the bank. Nope. He accidentally threw it away and found it in the trash later. We were too consumed with what came next. Finding real estate, getting equipment manufactured, and opening these locations was hot on our minds. That just showed how fast this train was running. By the way, we did get those checks deposited. In fact, we got a ton of checks deposited. We were a crackerjack leadership team that learned how to step up to any and every demand every single frantically busy day at Curves.

After the first year, as development skyrocketed, I decided that my office needed a better home than my bedroom. I rented a little office space in Waco and hired an assistant, CJ Bates. She was my very first employee at Curves. I had no idea what I was looking for; I just needed a worker bee to help me keep all of my ducks in a row. CJ looked like she was up to the task, so I hired her on the spot. I explained our little startup to give her background on the company I was growing. Of course, all she saw was a little three-room office. When she showed up for her second day of work, she said, "Well, I went home and told my husband I got this job. And he said, 'It sounds like some fly-by-night company.'" She was a country girl who spoke her mind. I knew we would get along perfectly. Her husband, Tommy, by the way, would eventually come to change his tune, too. As Curves grew over the coming years, he came to work for me, followed by CJ's son, her daughter-in-law, and even her son-in-law. They would all come to love this so-called fly-by-night organization. And, in the process, I would come to experience a corporate culture unlike any I had known before. Far from any business I had ever run or any organization I had ever worked at, Curves and its people would evolve into a second family for me.

CJ was a perfect example. Years into our working relationship, it dawned on me that CJ and her common-law husband had never enjoyed a proper wedding. They were two of the most loyal and loving people I knew. To me, that was deserving of a little celebration. Gary Heavin agreed with me. So we flew them to Las Vegas, paid for a fancy shindig, and Gary and I both escorted CJ down the aisle. They exchanged their vows, made it official, and became man and wife at a party we would never forget. That's the kind of company we were building. These were the kind of people we were employing. Much later, Gary and I would also speak at her husband's funeral. The love and care we had for our team members just never went away. CJ is more than 70 years old now, and she just recently retired working for me. Who would have guessed how long that journey would be when she became the first person on the inside about to witness a landslide of success?

Command central quickly became this three-room office in Waco. This is where we kept all the balls in the air. CJ was out front with an office on each side of her. I took one room for myself and I hired my second employee, an attorney named Kevin Ayers, for the other space. Kevin had worked for me at my health club while he put himself through Baylor Law School. As soon as he was done, I hired him to work at Curves. Our meager headquarters, however, was no match for the franchisees we were signing up. From the moment I started awarding deals, I needed a place in town to have new franchisee training events. These are the onboarding face-to-face meetings that franchisors host (usually at their big corporate campus) to prepare franchisees for running their businesses. That certainly wasn't going to happen out of my bedroom, and the three-room office that came next was no better.

Being the consummate salesman, I approached a local hotel. I explained the volume of visitors I was expecting in Waco, and I negotiated a fantastic deal. If I promised to give all of that business to the hotel, I wanted to use their meeting rooms for free in return. The manager agreed. Presto. I instantly had a training center for Curves.

Limited office space was one thing. Limited "Garys" were quite another. Gary and I could only be in so many places at one time. When we reached about 50 locations, he opened up an operations office in Tyler, Texas, and hired a former employee named Jane Manley to run it. We not only needed to grow the home team, but we also had to grow our field support as well. Gary set up a system where we began assigning mentors from existing locations to help with grand openings and site visits as more and more gyms were up and running. It was a genius move. If there was one tremendous advantage to the franchising business model, it was peer-to-peer best practices. Franchise owners not only benefited from what corporate delivered; they also benefited from these mentors who came from sister locations.

We identified strong employees of franchisees who came through training. Then we approached those franchise owners and asked if we could make those people mentors. We paid for those employees to go to other locations for one week a month and help with membership drives and strong openings. The franchisee was incentivized, and the mentor expanded his or her skills and grassroots experience by shaping business at Curves locations all over the map. At one point, when Curves had fully matured, we had as many as 400 mentors helping out in the field.

Our shoestring startup was looking all kinds of professional. We celebrated a magic milestone when Curves opened its 100th location. We were no longer newbies at this franchise game. We were a recognizable force in both the fitness and franchise industries. Compared to other franchise opportunities, it felt like it happened in the blink of an eye. At the same time, we started earning a lot of eyeballs now that we were more visible in our markets. Once franchisees had a taste of success, they started coming back for more. We quickly expanded to include many multi-unit owner operators. Franchisees who had success with one Curves gym wanted a second and then a third. At the same time, I knew from my days at The Dwyer Group that our corporate team had to grow as well to continue supporting our growing franchise network.

After we surpassed 100 locations, Gary promoted me to president. I, in turn, got busy expanding our staff and our office space in Waco. We bought a building in town and remodeled it. This was one of the first ways I paid back my buddy Gordon Swanson from my University Fitness days. With his help as the contractor, we now had an accounting team, a legal department, and training that we moved over from the hotel, all under one roof. We quickly realized our training facility, which could host 50 people, was too small. I called Gordon again, and he built an addition to the back that could host a couple hundred folks at once. Curves was really taking shape.

I never really knew how big we would get and neither did Gary. I did know that Rainbow had been around for more than a decade at The Dwyer Group and had reached 1,000 locations. It was my natural instinct to compare Curves against that. I figured if we ever got Curves to 1,000 sites, that would be a pretty good run. Meanwhile, we were already growing way faster than Rainbow ever did. At that rate, we had some things to figure out that I wasn't sure anybody in franchising had done before.

The early milestones were very big deals. We celebrated at

100, then 250, and soon 500 gyms. Each time was like a major historical achievement. After we reached 1,000, I think we quit counting. We were just doing our thing. And there were so many fandangled ways we did it, too. Oftentimes, I'm just glad we lived to tell it at all.

At least my trailer days were behind me when our brand began to mature. Luckily, we had grown our support staff to hand those equipment delivery duties off to others. When we got massively big, we even had an 18-wheeler to do the heavy lifting. Meanwhile, expanding our network farther across the country also meant upgrading my mode of transportation because I was spending so much time behind the wheel. Gary had a pilot's license and his own twin-engine plane. When the Curves franchise network started going national, Gary decided we should take to the air and keep pushing things along. To put it bluntly, that first plane was a lot like our first trailer. If it had 30 gauges on it, I swear that only 10 of them worked.

We flew that tin can through some of the craziest weather and landed at some of the smallest, two-bit airports. We aborted landings more often than I want to admit, but it was all in the name of our fast-rising star called Curves. One time in Scottsdale, Arizona, a guy at the front of the plane didn't close the door all the way. We went to take off and the door flew open. We had barely enough runway in front of us for an emergency landing. We got the door closed and, before we could comprehend our luck, we were back in the air and on to our next stop. On that same trip, we went to a meeting in Flagstaff, stayed on schedule, were back at the airport, and ready to head out. It was standard practice to look at the area radar screens at these airports before boarding, and we noticed some pretty serious storms up ahead. Gary said it was on the other side of Scottsdale. No problem. We could fly back to Scottsdale, refuel there, and decide our next move. Gary pointed to the radar and said, "You see that little hole right there (between two storms)? We can cut right through." My only reply was, "All I'm going tell you is this time of year is typhoon season. Nothing that starts out that way is going to stay that way." Gary, with his can-do attitude, said he still thought we could make it.

The captain had spoken. Gary, real estate guy John, and I quickly boarded the plane. I headed straight for the seat in the very back. I had a book in my hand and I figured, 'If I'm going to die, I'm going to die reading.' Once we got in the air, I was trying to mind my own business when I heard Gary tell John, "Well, I guess I should have listened to Gary." I peered over my book and looked through the front windshield. The sky was pure black in front of us. Gary looped around and, fortunately, we were over this little town, Casa Grande. We landed as fast as possible, jumped out of the plane, and hightailed it to a hotel to beat the storm. In the morning, when we woke up and headed back to the plane, it looked like Armageddon. The storm that blew through town had snapped giant telephone poles in half like toothpicks on both sides of the road. We didn't talk about our close call too much, but we did learn to appreciate radar readings more.

In many cases, we even became our own human radar detectors when needed. After so many trips in the clouds, I evolved into a veteran plane spotter and an extra set of eyes for precaution. We flew with very limited technology in those days. Still, I could hear the air traffic control tower say, "Beachcraft 1-2-2-3 Zulu," and I knew that was our tail number. Then, if he said, "You've got another plane at 10,000 feet," here I was, a self-proclaimed co-pilot looking for a plane headed right toward us. One time, all of a sudden, there it was. I yelled, "There they go." They were so close, I could dang near read the side of their plane. The tower was supposed to keep planes at least a mile apart. But when we were in that aircraft, sometimes it felt like 20 feet, sending shivers down my spine. Not to worry, though. We were like a couple of cowboys in the sky who didn't have time to dwell on a near miss. There would be plenty more where those came from.

One time we were headed to Wisconsin to a tiny airstrip. Our business model was still focused on small towns, and this was the nearest place to land for our next target market. It was right before dusk, and we were circling and circling the area, looking for this municipal airport. The place was full of trees and we couldn't find the runway. Adding to the anxiety? This tiny airport didn't have any runway lights. We were cutting it close on fuel and about to be in a world of hurt if we didn't find it soon. That's when I looked up and said, "Hey, look there." Right in front of us, a man in a parachute was falling steadily down to the ground. The tower knew we were having such a hard time that they had another plane take off and drop this guy in a parachute to show us the way. We circled behind him and followed him down to land.

That was almost as bad as another trip we made to a small-town airport only to fly around in a sea of darkness. We had to actually call, wake the tower up, and have them send someone down to turn on the runway lights. If I hadn't been a country boy from Axtell, Texas, I might have had a different opinion of those people in all of those little towns. Instead, I had a soft spot for those folks who operated on little sleep with too many duties and hardly any thanks in return. They were the fabric that kept those communities together.

The best close call by far was on a flight I wasn't even supposed to take. Gary phoned me up and said, "I've got to run to Arkansas and meet with a guy for about an hour. Come and go with me." I said no. My daughter Whitney had a game that night. "Oh, we'll be back in time. Just run up there with me," he said. His ability to talk me into something was never ending. I gave in, told Kim I had a plane to catch, and promised to be back lickety-split.

By now, Gary had traded up to plane number two, an Aerostar. I didn't like it because this aircraft's make and model had been involved in so many accidents it had earned the nickname the "Air-o-death." Gary didn't care. He had to buy one because it was the fastest twin-engine plane on the market before pricing up to the jet category.

As soon as we took off from the airport, Gary went to cycle up the landing gear and it wouldn't go up. I immediately told him to leave it alone because, if it didn't go up, it might not come down, either. I said, "Let's turn around, go back and land. You need to fix the problem." Well, that's not Gary's style at all. He couldn't leave it alone. He wanted to keep messing with it, and he did until the landing gear went up. Then he went to cycle it back down and, sure enough, the control panel wasn't showing anything. It could have engaged, but the indicator didn't read that the landing gear was locked in place. I could only imagine the look on my face

I credit my dad for giving me the entrepreneurial bug. He had his own business, the white-collar exception in a small town that showed me both the responsibilities and freedoms of being a boss. When it came to his kids, he also never missed a football game, a baseball game or rodeo appearance. I saw that work-life balance and knew I wanted it for myself.

Me and my blue ribbon pride and joy, Miss Syria Manso, took top honors at the State Fair of Texas. I was a kid who learned how to raise a champion and, for the first time in my life, a 1000-pound animal showed me I could conquer big goals.

I graduated from employee to business owner at a young age when I got to own and operate my own health club. That forever changed my love for the role of being a boss. I've embraced being a job creator, a team builder, a business leader and a champion for communities ever since.

I fell in love with my high school sweatheart, Kim Findley, and to this day say that I out punted my coverage. She has been the absolute best partner by my side with never-ending love and support for our family. There is no better advantage in life than somebody who believes in you.

I had the great honor of driving George Bush around town during his campaign stop in Waco in his race to become the Governor of Texas. He thanked me with his tickets to the next Texas Rangers baseball game. That generosity turned into a no-hitter and double the memories of our next governor and soon-to-be U.S. president.

One of the best business lessons I learned came from my years in the fitness industry — both as an independent owner/operator and in growing a global fitness franchise. Being the first to market or the cheapest with pricing is not as important as many people think. True staying power for a business comes down to how you treat your team and your customers.

Curves was a founder's dream and franchising the business became my exciting reality. When Gary Heavin asked me to look at his concept, a handshake deal turned into the ride of my life. There were three corporate-owned locations when I started and more than 8,000 franchise locations by the time I retired.

When the entire first floor of my home flooded, a restoration company not only saved our property but the harmony in our lives. That's why I jumped at the chance to run Restoration 1 when the opportunity came along and added bluefrog Plumbing + Drain as a natural extension a few years later. Dirty jobs deserve respect like no other.

I moved Restoration 1 headquarters from Florida to Texas in true redneck style, horses and all. Then it was off to the races with award-winning expansion for one brand and the ultimate dream to extend into multiple brands for home services. Today, Stellar Brands includes Restoration 1, bluefrog Plumbing + Drain, The Driveway Company and Softroc that prove, without a doubt, everything is bigger in Texas!

Today, I spend as much time talking about how to responsibly grow companies as I do actually growing them. That's the happy ending of sorts when a reputation for awarding more than 10,000 franchise agreements gets tagged to one's name. And I take the responsibility seriously, because each and every person running a franchise organization is in a position to help make someone's biggest dreams a real possibility.

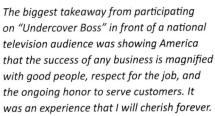

The biggest takeaway from participating on "Undercover Boss" in front of a national television audience was showing America that the success of any business is magnified with good people, respect for the job, and the ongoing honor to serve customers. It was an experience that I will cherish forever.

The term great outdoors will never be lost on me. I wear my redneck title with pride, and time at my ranch is proof that hard work truly does pay off in ways too beautiful to describe. There are two things that you cannot put a price on in my book: the time you have with family and the home you make together to share that love. My ranch is the ultimate reward to enjoy both.

sitting next to him. I said, "I told you so."

Since we couldn't see underneath the plane, we were instructed by the control tower to conduct a flyover at Waco Regional Airport. They had to have a guy in another plane fly underneath us to at least confirm that the landing gear appeared to be down. That much looked good. But without the indicator showing that it was locked in place, we still weren't out of the woods. We were instructed to fly around and give the airport enough time to place fire trucks at the end of the runway. Meanwhile, Gary told me, "Hey, climb back there. I've got some manuals and you can see if there's anything in there about this." I climbed to the back of the plane, found the manuals, and did the quickest read on emergency landings. I heard him get on the radio and say, "Okay, I'm going in for a landing." As soon as the wheels touched the ground, I prepared to cut off the fuel and pull the power back if needed. That way, if the plane caught on fire, at least it might not blow up on us.

We landed. Nothing exploded. We were alive. All was well. Arkansas would have to wait. Later, we found out a light had malfunctioned. Through that adrenaline rush, however, it never crossed my mind that I might be getting ready to die. Instead, we just pulled together and figured out how we could live. My first reaction after my feet were back on solid ground was to call Kim and tell her all about it.

I got her on the phone and said, "You're not going to believe this. We thought we were going to crash, and we landed the plane, and fire trucks were at the end of the runway...." I was talking 100 miles per hour.

Any other wife would be distressed and ask, "Oh, no! Are you all right?" Kim, however, was still the woman who never worried. She said, "Oh, okay. Talk to me when you get home. I've got to run the kids to baseball." That, in a nutshell, was the perfect response to how fast business was moving, how quickly life threw us curveballs, and how instinctively we just kept right on charging forward. With any other cast of characters in business and in life, I'm positive the Curves sensation would have been over before it began. Instead, here were these Texans who simply didn't know any better. It was always nose to the grindstone, and some way, somehow we finagled a gigantic success. I'll credit that to hard work and an equally powerful yet underestimated surefire way to get the word out.

Gary's gut instinct to keep Curves under the radar and growing quickly so we could own the marketplace was admirable. But these were small towns all across America. I'm pretty sure there's an 11th commandment somewhere that says, "Thou shalt not keep a secret in a small town." Friends would tell friends, and our phone would start ringing. Families who became franchisees had relatives, and soon a cousin needed to own one. Buddies got to talking, and now Curves sounded like a sure thing they all needed to join.

One of our multi-unit franchisees was in Paducah, Kentucky. I think this husband and wife had four daughters. Before I knew it, each one had her own Curves franchise to manage.

I had a retired doctor, Doc Roby, from Natchez, Mississippi, who was a franchisee. He later became one of my sales guys and a very close friend, too. I can still hear him on the phone talking with that Mississippi accent: "Gary, I bought this to give me something to do, and now it's done gone and given me a tax problem." He was a hoot. One time he was driving somewhere, and he had four buddies from church in the car with him. He got to telling them his Curves story and, the next thing you know, all four of them called us and bought franchises.

Some days, it just felt like a free-for-all. We got to where we could award 10 deals in a single day. People of a certain age might appreciate this analogy. But sometimes it felt like a run on cabbage patch dolls on Christmas Eve. That's how crazy people got about buying into our system. I even had people send checks to me for $100,000 and $200,000, saying they wanted 10 or 20 territories, and we had just started talking.

I could trace the earliest hints of a shift in direction all the way back to that 100-location benchmark. Once we crossed over, we suddenly didn't have to explain our concept anymore. People just knew, and the leads started coming to us instead. That kind of demand required more salespeople, too. I began building a sales team with a very different approach to the training I received at The Dwyer Group. First, people were all going to be contract employees. Everyone could work from home. Nobody had to come into some office to prove they were going to kill it every day. I made them all straight commission and, given the hot-as-it-gets nature of our franchise opportunity from the start, they didn't need any more incentive than that to close deals. From the very beginning at Curves, it wasn't about long hours, dream boards, and hard work. It was about excitement, great paydays, and teamwork. The end result was an incredibly happy group made up of friends and family, success like they'd never had before, and a record-setting number of new franchisees month after month, year after year. In the same way that Gary wanted to share a good thing with other passionate owner/operators, I wanted to share a good thing with the best salespeople on the planet. It was a win-win. And here's how it worked...

In the early days, we didn't have a lot of cash, but the word about Curves was getting out. Don Buster, a friend from SMI, approached me. He said, "Look, I don't have any money." I thought, no problem, neither did we. "But I do have credit cards," he said. I told him, "Okay. That's good. You can become a salesperson for me, and here's how it could work. You pay all of your own expenses. You run your own ads. Every expense you have is yours. You'll be an independent contractor. But for that, you can get 20 percent of any sale and an additional 20 percent of royalties perpetually for every franchise for as long as it's open." No doubt, Don was taking a risk. We hadn't done too much to brag about yet, but I think he went on to sell about 3,000 franchise locations. On top of the commission with each sale, that was another $80 per deal for a $400 royalty each year. In essence, Don took home another $240,000 after the sale each year at the height of his run with Curves.

Another guy I invited onto my sales team was my dad. After our gym had failed, he filed bankruptcy and then spent the better part of the next eight years being a serial entrepreneur. He was a great salesperson. Somehow he would make deals with little food companies that made fried pies or pecan pralines, and then he masterminded this route all over East Texas where he enlisted convenience stores that sold those goods at the counter. It wasn't like anything you could get from Nabisco or Sysco. Anyone who has ventured into a small-town country store in Texas knows exactly what I mean. He made a living out of this, and he and my mom still lived in the same house in Axtell where I grew up. But now well into his 50s, I wanted him to get more out of his great skills by coming to Curves. I told him, "Look, you know how to sell. You're just as good as anybody else. I want you to come onboard." He agreed, and like anybody else I hired, I took him on three or four sales calls to show him how it was done.

In true Findley style, our first trip together was about as redneck as you could get. My dad and I took a drive to Oklahoma. He was riding along with me when we made a stop in the town of West to get a kolache, the best Czech pastry in the world. This little city just north of Waco is famous for its Czechoslovakian bakeries, and people can't help themselves but pull off the interstate to get a kolache and coffee at the infamous Czech Stop. We got our pastries and got right back on the highway when, in the middle of the road, there was this huge piece of metal. I saw it at the very last minute. I couldn't go left, and I couldn't go right. So I drove right over this thing, and we heard it get stuck underneath the car. This enormous chunk of tin was wedged so tight that we got off on the access road and drove slowly over a bridge. We were planning to turn around and head the other way when we ended up smack-dab in front of this old trailer on the side of the road. You could hear us coming a mile away from the huge sound this grinding metal was making underneath our car, not to mention this long, deep groove we were cutting into the road behind us. As we came to a stop in front of this trailer, we were merely the latest addition to a mountain of scrap out in the front yard.

That's when a redneck came out from behind a screen door. He never said a word to us. He just looked at us, peered underneath the car, and turned around and walked back into the trailer. He reemerged with this little jack, jacked up our car with both of us inside, and reached under there and pulled out this hunk of metal. We didn't know what to make of it all. My dad and I just looked at him, said thanks, and waved as we drove away. That was our first burning memory together in the Curves franchise sales induction. Thankfully, the actual business part was much more professional and successful. We made it to Oklahoma, my dad heard me deliver the sales pitch to a prospect in person, and he picked it up in no time. As expected, dad became a real pro in franchise development. And unlike our first gym together, we each enjoyed another kind of success by expanding the Curves fitness network.

Once I had a good team of salespeople in place for domestic growth, it was time to look beyond the borders. I started attending franchise trades shows, and then I returned for big grand openings. English-speaking countries were the natural first step, so we expanded to places like Canada, the U.K., and Ireland at first. With each new international flag, I was a redneck on a cultural expedition. To the locals, I was also like a circus attraction. People could walk by my booth at a trade show, and they just naturally stuck around to listen to this guy with the strange Texas twang. Maybe they just wanted me to keep talking. In no time at all, I also had them buying franchises. I found a real passion for international travel with those Curves trips, and I also learned a lot about life outside of the Lone Star State.

When I hit Canada in the winter, I saw 40 below in the weather bulletin and almost turned back around. I wasn't worldly enough to know that other countries tracked weather in Celsius versus Fahrenheit. Nevertheless, I still braced against some harsh winters around the world. Then there was a special trip I made to our first grand opening in Ireland. A big celebration was scheduled with a ribbon cutting for their version of the local chamber of commerce. I lost my voice doing a radio interview when I first arrived the day before. When it came time for speeches at the actual shindig, I had to apologize to the crowd. I told everyone I felt a little under the weather, and all of these Irish attendees busted out laughing. Someone later explained to me that what I had said meant I was up late drinking all night. Even I got a chuckle. I could add one more stamp to my redneck passport of worldly wisdom.

This dance with franchise expansion across the globe managed to turn Curves into a legitimate worldwide phenomenon. We began celebrating our title as the world's fastest-growing franchise of any kind. We also rose to become the largest fitness chain on the planet, and that power and influence truly shined. We had made a conscious decision that we would not start national advertising until we reached 5,000 locations. Part of that was due to the fact that we had a flat marketing fee back then of $199 a month per gym. When you did the math, 5,000 locations equaled $1 million a month, and that was the kind of advertising budget that could get people talking. Suddenly, we went from complete silence to inviting some of the biggest advertising agencies in America for a chance to win the $12 million Curves advertising account. Big outfits doing creative for BMW, Chick-fil-A, and others lined up to pitch for the business. We had our pick of the litter from great talent and signed up with Publicis, a big agency in Dallas that did outstanding work. I was the president of a brand that had used a three-page marketing brochure to launch this franchise, and we now had one of the best advertising agencies in America putting Curves on TV, radio, and print from coast to coast.

Reveling in all that success was special for the Curves family. We worked hard, and over the years we learned to play hard, too. I once accepted a Harley Davidson as a down payment on a franchise, and I knew before the keys were in my hand what was ahead of me. It was the first of several Harleys I would own, and I wasn't alone. The entire executive team at Curves soon transformed from a group of thought leaders in the boardroom to a biker gang on the wide-open road. We made several cross-country rides to Sturgis, South Dakota, among other hot spots. When the money got really good, we just flew up there in the Curves plane and had the Curves 18-wheeler bring our bikes and gear.

Not to be outdone on the ground, we all got into hot-air balloon races, too. Gary and a couple of others on the leadership team were licensed to pilot balloons. So there we went. We hit remote towns in destinations across the country to do tactical races, a lot like scavenger hunts, with our hot-air balloons. Even when the International Balloon Festival in Albuquerque, New Mexico, was delayed due to weather one year, the Curves crew took to the air and threw caution to the wind. We were the perfect club of misfits who worked well together, both in and out of the office.

I could never have predicted that working hard and having fun would play out the way that it did. We made memories that would most definitely last me a lifetime while building our little franchise empire.

The best personal outcome of all that success, however, came in giving more than receiving. Gary and I were both strong Christians who were compelled to give. I watched him and Diane tithe a small fortune over the years to the poor, the hungry, nonprofits, missionary work, and more. Kim and I were cut from the same fabric. The minute we started making some real money, there was never a question that we would find important ways to share it. That included reimbursing old vendors after I went belly up, giving great jobs to people who had supported me in my past, and finding our own special ways to be philanthropic to causes and people who could benefit from our own good fortune.

On the business side, we asked Gordon Swanson to build us a brand-new house. Again, this was the same Gordon who said I didn't owe him a dime when the gym that he built at Baylor went under. He now had become a successful homebuilder, so we were grateful to give him the business. We traded up to another one of Gordon's new homes after that, and then he built us our dream home on a golf course. He built a new home for Gary and Diane Heavin, too. Before all was said and done, another three or four people from Curves were living in new homes built by Gordon.

That was followed by commercial jobs for Gordon. He built our 16,000-square-foot training center, which I thought would last us forever. Then it was time for a brand-new office building for our continually growing staff. I turned to Gordon and gave him a $5 million project to build a new corporate headquarters for Curves with 45,000 square feet of space, three boardrooms, and the capacity to onboard as many as 500 people at a time. Gary had only two demands for the building: First, pay in cash. Second, make sure his office was bigger than mine. Gordon and

I were the design team, and I would say without a shadow of a doubt we designed the most beautiful headquarters in McLennan County. With Curves sites reaching some 30 countries around the globe, we also needed separate rooms with training in multiple languages. We needed the technology and translators that could take our messages from a main stage and push it out across a global audience in breakout rooms. It was a revolutionary approach for the world's biggest fitness gym. Gordon took the job and performed to perfection.

Some eight years after it all began, I took some time to reflect. I had expanded a franchise organization from my bedroom to a 45,000-square-foot building. We went from three locations down by the Mexican border to 8,000 gyms around the world. I had gone from bankrupt to millionaire. Life as the Curves president was a ride like no other. I know the good Lord showered me with this success in more ways than I could have ever imagined. And now, for some strange reason, at the height of it all and without explanation, I woke up one day and decided I was ready to leave it all behind me. In January 2004, I went straight to the only person I ever talked to about my biggest business decisions. I walked into my kitchen one morning and told Kim I wanted to quit my job.

Perhaps there was nothing left for me to build. We had 8,000 gyms and a team to keep it all going. We had this beautiful building, and Gary and Diane had offices and were involved in a whole new way with the business. Gary had firm control of operations, Diane had a wonderful handle on marketing and advertising, and every team had a capable leader. I even had someone running development with 13 sales guys who were still making things happen. Everything was in place. The rate at which we were blowing and going was also starting to slow. We weren't selling 3,000 deals a year anymore. Maybe I could see change on the horizon. This women-only gym may have had its shining moment, but somehow I wasn't sure it would be the end-all for eternity. That was neither here nor there. Gary and Diane were committed to what they had built and, for some reason, I believed it was time for me to exit. I certainly had nothing else lined up. That wasn't my style. What did I need to do anyway? Maybe I was ready to retire.

I can look back now and see how crazy it must have sounded to Kim. It's like I said, "Honey, I made $3.2 million last year. I think I'm going to quit." It was a curve ball, for sure. And, no, I didn't say it like that. But it was certainly in a country boy matter-of-fact way. True to form, she took it all in stride. This woman who had stuck with me through thick and thin could somehow see my mind was made up. It was almost like there was peace for both of us about it. That didn't mean it would be so easy to tell Gary.

From the moment I made my decision, there was no time to dawdle. I knew I needed to tell Gary and Diane right away. I called them up and asked if Kim and I could come over. We needed to talk.

I was about to do one of the hardest things in my life. I never knew how tortured I would be inside. I physically had to walk around the block at my house a few times just to get right in my own head. I was preparing to tell the two people who had invited me into their lives and their business, cared for me and my family as their own, turned me into a millionaire, made me the president of their global brand, and had become my closest and dearest friends that I had to go.

Kim and I walked into their home, I shared my news, they both asked me if I was sure about my decision, and then it was final. Gary had months and months of international travel on his calendar for our growing network, so he asked me to stay on for another six months as I transitioned out of the company. No problem. Then he said he owed me my 10 percent of the value of the organization from our handshake deal eight years before. He figured Curves was worth about $100 million now. He said he would give me $10 million as promised. How did that sound? I said that sounded amazing. Always true to his word, Gary did exactly what he said he would do.

My last hurrah came at our international franchise convention that year in Las Vegas. We had more than 5,000 people in attendance. They played a wonderful tribute video to me from the stage, and I got a standing ovation. It was a humbling moment for the kid from Axtell, Texas. Gary and Diane said, "We have a gift for you." I have to admit I thought it was going to be a new motorcycle or chopper, but it was a rocking chair. This was the relationship we all had; we had a great time building one of America's fastest and largest fitness franchise companies. The real parting goodbye, however, was in true ragtag entrepreneurial fashion. Gary was actually out of the country on my last official day at the office. He called me up to say goodbye, said he wished he could do it in person, and then told me to go down to accounting and have them cut me my check.

The accounting department cut a check for $10 million. I was the only executive who could sign it. Go figure. On my last day of work for Curves, I signed a check made out to me for $10 million and then officially left the company.

I was 43 years old and now an unemployed multimillionaire.

Life Lesson: Never give up on your dream. It's never left you; it's just sometimes on hold. Work for people you trust, admire and, above all, have integrity. Life really is short in the scheme of things, so do your best to love what you do.

8

IT AIN'T OVER TIL THE COWS COME HOME

Mark Twain famously said, "The two most important days in your life are the day you are born and the day you find out why." As my professional career took off in my 30s and 40s, I still constantly looked for the *why* in my life. I had proven myself as a business success by most standards. I had grown the Curves franchise network into a global brand. I had reaped the riches of hard work. In the process, I had focused on ways to stay grounded in my faith and the common sense that I had carried since my childhood. Yet there had to be more.

The day I left Curves, Kim and I took $2 million from my golden parachute and started The Findley Foundation. It was time to step up our charitable activities. Who knows, maybe I was taking myself to a whole new place as well.

###

While at Curves, I constantly sought self-improvement. It wasn't hard to have an ego running the day-to-day operations of the top fitness franchise in the world, but I never considered myself the smartest man in the room by a long shot. Heck, I only had a two-year degree from a community college. If I had a moment to spare, I needed to make up for what that schoolboy from Axtell School lacked. I embraced what made this country boy successful, but I also questioned my higher purpose. That's when I became a voracious reader. Suddenly I had one, two, or three books on my nightstand at all times.

I read all kinds of books. Business books, motivational books, Christian books, and biographies were all part of my self-assembled library at home. I studied how Sam Walton created Walmart, how Truett Cathy launched Chick-fil-A, how Fred DeLuca formed Subway, and what they did with that success. I read biographies of famous politicians like Ronald Reagan. I studied the conscious capitalism of Howard Schultz at Starbucks. Books became my obsession and my continuing education. Meanwhile, their messages constantly struck a chord in one way or another as I regularly evaluated my own station in life. I would come to understand in my own way that, yes, it was absolutely wonderful to have money, and lots of it. Because of Curves, we could put our kids through college, enjoy nice vacations, buy fancy toys, and live in nice houses. But something more had to come from hard work than just easy living. It was a constant and ever-growing journey for me.

That's where Christian books fed a very special need. I read fantastic Christian books by Chuck Swindoll, Rick Warren, and others. Then one day, on a long drive to Colorado, I popped in an audiobook by an author named Patrick Morley. It was called "The Man in the Mirror: Solving the 24 Problems Men Face." I was on a trip for Curves in the early days of the company's development and my life, not to mention my job, was running nonstop. This book could not have landed in front of me at a better time. Its message and the ability to be grounded in a world that was pulling me in so many different directions were transformative. It was compelling to me not only for where I was at that very moment, but where I was headed next and how I wanted to live my life along the way. I had constantly chased money and the dream of being wealthy. At that time, I hadn't found it yet. In my state of mind, I'm not sure how I would have handled it if I did. That book and the ability to see past money's fleeting gifts made all the difference in what I was called to do. I had a new frame of mind about my family, my life, my job, and my surroundings. I obsessed less about the bottom line and more on how it could empower me to help others.

Throughout the mounting success of our franchise network, it wasn't a matter of what I could buy, but what I could give, that made the stronger impression. Listening to that book on tape turned into one of the most successful drives I ever took. I would recall it over and over, and I applied its message in theory and practice to my life in ways that have influenced my decisions ever since.

For as far back as I could remember, I always focused on a need to be successful. All I knew was that I wanted to make money. "The Man in the Mirror" helped me start to see beyond the dollar signs. I still recall the day, after some pretty hefty paychecks came my way, I went out and bought Kim a shiny new BMW 750i. It was the nicest thing on the road. I gave it to her, she drove it one week, and then she took it back and traded it in for a Suburban. That other thing was way too showy. To be honest, she said she was embarrassed to be seen in it. She still drove a very nice car, but not one that called anyone's attention. Okay, I got it. I didn't need to buy something only because I could. These were the remnants from my dream-board days at The Dwyer Group with a leader who parked a Rolls Royce by the front door. Quite frankly, God had already pointed out more than once, "If materialistic things are all that matter to you, let me just take it all away to make my point." Instead, I really needed to focus more on my family, my relationships with others, my relationship with God, and what kind of person I could be. I gladly welcomed that lesson, and I began to set my own personal goals on how to trade the rat race for a more authentic life. Life after Curves allowed me to explore that on a whole new level.

Decades into my marriage, Kim still remained the saver and I was the spender. One common ground was a need for both of us to be charitable. From the time Kim was a child, she had always wanted to be a missionary. She entered this world with a big heart for helping others. Then she grew up poor in a little copper mining town in Arizona, and constantly looked for ways to give back. Everyone in town worked at the mine and, for the most part, were on the same financial scale. Falling in love with me, however, wasn't in Kim's master plan. After we got married, she realized she would never be a missionary living in Mexico. That didn't mean she couldn't give. Our family went on mission trips through our church. Then Kim found an outreach group in San Marcos that went on regular trips into Mexico to build homes for the poor. She followed along on an adventure, saw a whole new level of poverty and hunger up close, and from that moment we regularly contributed to the effort that constructed casitas across the border. Those small houses weren't much by American Dream standards, but they were everything to homeless families across the border who rummaged through the city dump to stay alive. Now an entire community of gingerbread houses in Easter-egg colors blankets the landscape, providing roofs over people's heads and places to house donated beds and belongings.

Kim was a constant source of inspiration to find ways like that to make a lasting impact. It rubbed off on our children, too. Micah was in middle school when he noticed that his friend, whose parents were missionaries, was picked up in the family's rundown minivan. Then Kim rolled up in her new Suburban. Micah hopped in and told Kim, "Boy, I sure feel bad for them. All they do is help everybody else, and it's people like that who have to drive around in crappy cars." We knew them very well. They were good friends of ours. Yet, our son, a middle-school kid, saw something we hadn't even noticed. Kim came straight home and told me all about it. A couple of weeks later, his buddy came up to him at school and gave him a big hug. Micah was clueless. His friend said, "You didn't know?" That's when Micah found out that we had gone out and bought them a new minivan. Micah tells that story to this day, knowing what it means to be a good steward with one's success.

I found my own outlets through my service projects, too. I served on the board of Mission Waco where we made regular contributions to feed the hungry and support the poor through the charity's endeavors. Then one day it dawned on me that Jimmy Dorrell, the co-founder and president of Mission Waco, could also use a helping hand. I went to those board meetings, and I started to notice that Jimmy would run late because of car trouble. If he couldn't be where he needed to be, how could Mission Waco go where it needed to go? I talked to Kim and we decided not to ask. We just went ahead and did it. I called up Jimmy one day while Kim and I were in Dallas. I said I needed his driver's license number and told him not to ask any questions. Without warning, one week before Christmas, Kim and I pulled up to his house and delivered a new Toyota Tacoma and handed him the keys. We told him not to tell anyone where he got it, just keep doing the good work he was meant to do. He needed a trustworthy vehicle, and we needed Mission Waco's president to have one less headache. With reliable transportation, he could concentrate on what needed his attention the most. I never had a Christmas that felt so good.

Another bucket-list item was using The Findley Foundation to give someone a home. In good times and bad, I knew firsthand how important it was to have a roof over my head. I also knew what an incredible feeling it was to live in a new house. I wasn't sure when, where, how, or why, but I wanted to pay it forward. Once again, my time on the board for Mission Waco shined a light where I could see it. The board was full of prominent local business leaders, except for one reserved seat. Jimmy, the president, made the very wise decision to always fill a board position with a true member of Waco's less fortunate. That person could be the eyes and ears of life among the needy for those of us who were further removed from that community. That's how I was blessed to meet an African-American woman named Brenda Shepherd. Brenda lived in the projects in Waco. The first time Kim and I met her, I think we took her some gifts one Christmas, and I distinctly remembered she had a chain with a lock on her refrigerator. That was so people wouldn't steal her food or eat anything that was meant to last a lot longer. Brenda had a heart of gold. She was helping raise her niece's children while her niece served time in prison. She also was dealing with her own health setbacks, going to dialysis every week and battling cancer. Brenda had a lot of cards stacked against her, but she absolutely lived life to the fullest. She always brought a smile and positive energy to our board at Mission Waco, too. One day at a board meeting, Brenda told a story about how she had always wanted to own her own house. She dreamed of one day owning a small home with a little front porch. I'm sure her message was more about us understanding that even poor people could have dreams. They don't always have to see themselves as stuck forever. She made a casual remark that, "Before I die, I want my own house."

It was another one of those light-bulb moments. Kim and I talked about it, and we wanted to make Brenda's dream come true. We talked to Jimmy and told him our plan. Nobody but Brenda would need to know about it. To everyone else, it could just be some anonymous donors who worked through Mission Waco to make it all happen. Jimmy thought it was a wonderful idea. He even got the City of Waco to donate the lot. It was the perfect little piece of land with a huge tree out front just a few blocks from Antioch Baptist Church. Kim and I got some architectural plans drawn up and reviewed them with Brenda. We enlisted some friends to donate time and energy in sweat equity. The Findley Foundation footed the bill for the rest. I will never forget the day when Mission Waco hosted a ribbon-cutting ceremony outside of the cutest three-bedroom house with a porch on the front. The newspaper even showed up and wrote a nice story. After that, when Kim and I would visit on occasion, Brenda kept a little framed picture of us inside. She called us her guardian angels. Kim and I didn't need any kind of credit for this gesture from the outside world. We just wanted Brenda to realize her hopes and dreams.

Six months later, Kim and I attended the annual Mission Waco banquet. The organization hosted it every year as a fundraiser, which attracted hundreds of people. Brenda was a fixture at the event each time, so Kim and I looked for her to say hello as everyone was directed to their tables. I remember all of us looking around. We were all asking, "Where's Brenda?" Oh well, the show was starting. We had to be seated.

Finally, Jimmy walked up on stage before the festivities were set to begin with an announcement. He said he had some sad news. He just wanted everyone to know that many of us knew and loved Brenda Shepherd but, unfortunately, he had learned that she had passed away. Someone had gone to her house to give her a ride to the banquet and found that she had succumbed to her cancer. She was inside her home, and she could not be revived. It hit me and Kim like a ton of bricks. I was stunned. I was speechless. In a split second, I was also so relieved that she did not leave this earth without experiencing her one biggest wish. Before she died, she did indeed have her own house. However short it lasted, she could have that memory forever. I think her relatives inherited the property, which was fine by us. That home had already served its mission. It was just one of many lasting impacts we wanted to make, and someone up above reminded us how short our time was to do so.

Alongside making some money, I learned another very important lesson. You could take the boy out of the country, but you couldn't take the country out of the boy. As I gained some success, I looked for ways to invest, and soon enough Kim and I bought a nice piece of land for a ranch. It was 27 acres with a small cabin. It also had a barn with an apartment and horse stalls, not to mention plenty of God's best work to look at in every direction as far as the eyes could see. It was a regular gathering spot for family and friends. We enjoyed numerous weekends hunting, fishing, and getting away from the daily grind. During my Curves days, we would bus people from franchise training out there for a good, old-fashioned Texas barbecue. Many of them had never even seen cows or horses up close. It was a peaceful escape, and it butted up against a gorgeous stretch of 350 acres owned by the Camp Fire Girls. We admired that neighboring property from afar. After I retired form Curves, a little rumor came our way.

The Camp Fire Girls had been given that land in the 1960s. They then borrowed money against the property and couldn't make the payments. A huge sanctuary was about to be lost to the highest bidder. Before the news was public, Kim and I decided to make an offer for the place from The Findley Foundation. It would become our single biggest charitable investment. The minute it came into our possession, we started fixing up the place. It needed a ton of work. It had cabins, a cafeteria, a swimming pool, tennis courts, a basketball court, and a riding program that all needed updating. We got the place in beautiful shape. Shortly after, we were approached to host a therapeutic horseback-riding program for disabled kids. That prompted us to add a really wonderful barn to the place. We hosted summer camps there. We let ministries use the place. Mission Waco even hosted Easter services and used the river to baptize people. That piece of land became a gift to so many wonderful groups. It also taught me that my love for land and the great outdoors growing up was something that so many others could now appreciate, too. And the word got out.

Micah was out on the property one day, working on the mower when a guy drove up in a flatbed Dodge 3500 truck. He stopped and said, "Is Gary here?" Micah said, "No, sir. I'm his son." He said, "Okay. I want to give this to you all." He handed Micah the keys to the truck. He added, "I know the good things y'all are doing out here, and this is an old farm truck that may come in handy." Micah had no clue who the guy was. It reminded him of that minivan we had given our friends, the missionaries. He said, "I remembered in that moment that what goes around comes around."

When I decided to leave Curves, I had the perfect opportunity to do something that was long overdue. I went back to college to get my four-year degree. I enrolled at the University of Mary Hardin-Baylor in Belton, Texas. My book smarts had some catching up to do. It wasn't so much about what school could teach me; it was more about what I could teach my youngest son. Something told me I might regret never finishing college if I hoped for my children to go. That's not to say that college is for everyone. It's not. Some kids are better suited for other careers. Some kids are automatically driven to go to college. Others are great candidates who might need convincing. I needed to be prepared.

As fate would have it, I'd raised very hard workers in the Findley clan, and one was a next-generation entrepreneur. Micah was in high school during my time at Curves, and his strong work ethic (like that of all of my children) was showing huge promise. I had invested in some duplexes and apartment properties around town, and I hired a friend with a landscaping business to handle all of the yard work for them. That friend turned around and was paying Micah $8 an hour to be part of his crew. It took my kid a hot minute to figure out he could skip the middleman.

When he was just 14, Micah enlisted his cousin, and they did what any number of hard-working teenagers would do to earn a buck. They began mowing lawns. Unlike their peers, they were doggone ambitious about it, too. This became far more than just soliciting the neighbors where we lived. They weren't old enough to drive, so they hired buddies with a driver's license to drive them to jobs and grow their client base even further.

As soon as Micah got his license, the boys began mowing the lawn at Curves headquarters. While they were there, they talked to all of the Curves employees and added another 30 lawns to their list. I agreed to pay for half of Micah's first riding lawnmower, too, so I could use it out at my ranch. I'll be danged if these boys didn't build one heck of a landscaping business all on their own.

By the time Micah was a senior in high school, he and his cousin had four employees. The business had two crews; trucks, trailers, and equipment that were all paid for; and a steady list of 200 lawns on the books. Micah was on a work-release program and only went to school until 10 a.m. every day. They wouldn't let him use his own landscaping business though. As part of the criteria for the school program, he had to be an employee with a pay stub from a third party. Pretty crazy, huh? Micah literally had to give me money through his landscaping business to pay him back with a pay stub. The teachers even knew what he was doing.

Micah and a buddy showed up to school with mower trailers on their trucks. His older cousin and another buddy had already graduated and were out doing lawns all day. Micah would join them for the rest of the day, go back to school at 3 p.m., and pick up his best friend Jay, who he also recruited to the business. They all pocketed some great money. In fact, that company is still up and running today and has some original customers from when the boys first started.

When it was time to go to college, Micah sold the business outright to his cousin. College was a tricky proposition though. By the look of things, this business owner was doing just fine, and he hadn't even turned 18. I knew exactly what that felt like. I was working on the railroad and making some pretty good cash at that age. That was one of the biggest reasons why I had to go back and finish college P-D-Q. I had to be able to make the argument when Micah needed to move on.

In the fall of 2004, after I left Curves, I became a student again and enrolled at the University of Mary Hardin-Baylor. I knew the campus well. I had made countless visits over the years at the invitation of business professors to come and speak to students about Curves and franchising. The professors became good friends. The students were exceptional, too. So I eventually occupied a desk like the rest of them on my way to finishing my bachelor's degree. On my very first day as a student, I was in a marketing class when I opened the textbook and saw the first chapter was all about Curves. I should make an "A" in this class, I thought.

Time flew by. The drive to and from Belton for classes was a breeze. I even started another business during all of this. Finally, on December 16, 2006, I crossed the stage. I was 44 years old and an official college graduate. I felt led to do this, and all of the pieces finally fell into place.

As a parting gesture to the institution, Kim and I made a $75,000 donation from The Findley Foundation toward the construction of Manning Chapel as part of the Paul and Jane Meyer Christian Studies Center. I hoped that countless students would continue to benefit in whatever little way we contributed to this special place.

What the school gave me in return had no price tag and was far more valuable. When it was time for my youngest son to take the plunge and go to college, his dad had plenty of opinions about getting it done. Thank goodness he did.

Life Lesson: Success is not about wealth and possessions. It is about the positive impact you can make in the world and on those around you. Being charitable, bettering myself in ways outside of a traditional job, and leading by example have all been equally important journeys for me. Live your life with the desire to help others and you will make a difference. Happiness and peace cannot be bought.

9

FRANCHISING'S FREE AGENT

If somebody would have told me that one day I would have more than $10 million and nothing but time on my hands, the younger Gary Findley might have seen that as a final victory. Then reality hit that I had $10 million and nothing but time on my hands. After a few lazy days at home with the prospect of infinitely more, I figured out in a big hurry that it wasn't all it was cracked up to be. More specifically, when you've worked hard your whole life, not working at all hardly comes naturally. Not to worry. I was officially retired from Curves for a whopping two weeks at best when my phone rang with a proposition.

Two Curves franchise owners had an idea for another venture, and for some reason they wanted my opinion. They were helping fund a business that their two girlfriends dreamed up. This particular business would offer nothing but facials, and they would call it Facelogic. They saw a huge market of opportunity to take this concept far and wide and, because of their experience as Curves franchisees, they wanted to franchise it from the start. So, what did I think? Hmm. My curiosity was all theirs.

That was followed by another inquiry. This time, a real estate buddy in Waco wanted me to check out a local small business that was teaching cooking skills to children. Could I come down and look at it? The entrepreneur behind this cooking school for kids thought it might make a good franchise. Okay, I would look it over.

Then came another call. And then another. My free and easy "I'm retired" calendar started filling up with all kinds of appointments from all sorts of different people. Everyone wanted franchising advice. If I had solidified a reputation for doing anything well, it was growing the Curves franchise network to 8,000 locations in eight years. The minute I left the team, it was like I became some kind of hot free agent on NFL draft day. Apparently, my track record at Curves made me an attractive commodity to a whole string of franchising dreamers who were ready to go big with their brands.

Once again, when I had nothing on the horizon after my past gig, a road of opportunity presented itself. There was one itty-bitty problem. I wasn't the least bit interested in working for anyone. Don't get me wrong, it sure felt good to feel needed, but I was one of the highest paid presidents in town at my old job. My final year on the payroll, I took home a generous annual salary of $3.2 million with a parting gift of $10 million. Why on earth would I want to answer to somebody else as an employee they literally couldn't afford? As we say in the South, that dog don't hunt.

There was only one way to do this. Well, only one way that would hold my interest.

If I could counsel multiple people from multiple companies, that would be a role worth pursuing. I decided I had enough money and enough knowledge to take one more gigantic entrepreneurial leap in life. I became a founder for the very first time of my own business. In the fall of 2005, I opened The Findley Group. This company would do one thing that everyone seemed to be wanting. It would help entrepreneurs, start-ups, and franchisors turn their business ideas into growing franchise networks. It would guarantee access to the development guy: me. My services would transfer the skills I gathered at Curves over to clients who retained The Findley Group in search of the same expertise.

From the outside looking in, that's the justification I gave myself on day one for launching into this new adventure. However, it wasn't the only reason I decided that I wanted to go back to work. Another interesting thing happened when I left the team at Curves. The key players that I had assembled during my time there had lost their coach. Coincidentally, one of the attorneys on the executive team who wasn't my biggest fan decided that he wasn't all that interested in keeping the same roster. I started getting word that great people, my people, were getting pushed out at Curves. Then others straight up wanted to leave. These were sales guys, support staff, and friends who felt like my second family when, together, we built the Curves culture that became so successful and fun.

Now, nothing was fun about what I was hearing after I left. So, imagine if I had a place where they could come instead. I considered it a stroke of luck that some brands wanted franchising advice at the same time that several people at Curves were searching for a new assignment. Just like that, we slowly got the band back together. Over the next several months, I hired eight of my key employees from Curves. Being the generous and now considerably more comfortable executive that I was, I made the impractical decision to start them at their current salaries from over at Curves. For all of you playing along, that means that these individuals who were supporting a franchise network of 8,000+ locations at Curves would get the same pay to come and work for me in an unproven attempt to expand several no-name brands. As a first-time founder, my cup runneth over. However, at these salaries, it would also eventually go bone dry.

I went out and bought a building on New Road in Waco. We remodeled the space, and it was my new corporate headquarters. Our first three clients were Facelogic, a cooking school for kids, and Nanny Poppins (a nanny service out of Florida). Then we made the rounds at franchise trade shows, representing all these brands at once. It was a bold new step in the franchise development space for companies to outsource this function to The Findley Group. We not only left those shows with interested prospects looking to invest in these brands, but we also left with more clients. Every time we attended a show, we picked up one or two more brands on our way out the door.

To be clear, I never intended to encroach on someone else's existing franchise development business. The standard industry practice was to keep this function and a full-time sales team in-house. But when my name and our services at The Findley Group became well known, the business leads headed our way. One guy I knew was a broker who introduced me to two other guys at a franchise show. The broker was doing development for them and, before I even got back to my hotel room, they were calling me. They said, "Hey, we met you today. He's not doing a good job and we want you to do development for us." It was literally that fast.

We rapidly grew our client list over the next couple of years to include 12 franchise organizations looking to expand their footprints in a big way. We represented Romp n' Roll, a kids' activity center out of Virginia; Games2U, a mobile gaming center for children's birthday parties and special events; Dogtopia, a dog daycare and grooming chain; Bahama Bucks, the original shaved ice company; and many more. Two of the companies we represented even went on the TV show "Shark Tank" a few years later.

One of the most amazing things I learned when we really got going was how much fun a sales team could have when they had more than one franchise opportunity to share. A portfolio of franchise brands amped up a whole new level of excitement for development guys used to representing a single concept as their only way to make money. We were no longer an all-eggs-in-one-basket kind of growth group.

However, for some of our opportunities, we needed to perfect the prototype before we could go out and sell it. Unlike my start at Curves where Gary Heavin had already developed the concept and duplicated it, some of the brands approaching The Findley Group hadn't always graduated to that level. In the case of Facelogic, my very first client, I went out and built the first franchise to get it off the ground, which oddly enough is one of the few still open today in Waco. Then I structured the relationship for an equity position in the business and counseled the founders, former Curves franchisees who designed and funded the concept. I taught them everything they needed to know about franchising the business, from soup to nuts. This was right about the same time that Massage Envy was launching as a franchise. Similar to the Facelogic business model, this idea of monthly membership services for high-end things like massages and facials seemed to be gaining an audience. My intuition was right. The Findley Group awarded close to 100 franchise agreements for Facelogic in the first 18 months we supported the brand.

The kids cooking school played out in much the same way. When a friend asked me to tour a tiny 500-square-foot space where the owner was giving cooking classes to kids, I saw a delicious business concept, albeit in a very hungry location that needed a ton of help.

Again, I didn't just waltz into a business concept that was ready to franchise. I ended up investing money to get a good prototype off the ground so we could grow it. I had a buddy (Gordon, again) get us the commercial space he owned with no deposit up front. He built out the space to suit with a training room as well. We officially had an all-in-one storefront and franchise training space.

I would help market the opportunity, sell it, and also get a percentage of the royalties once a successful location, and hopefully many others, got going. I had a long-term play in mind that justified my willingness to help fund things in the beginning. When all of the ingredients were just right, The Findley Group awarded over 100 franchise agreements in the first 18 months for the concept.

One thing was for sure. The Findley Group could sell franchises. Over time, we helped some notable franchise opportunities gain serious ground. We were moving the needle. Maybe my sales guys were not doing the same numbers from their Curves days, but I was the eternal optimist. Heck, I gave out a Christmas bonus each year even when we were losing money. And, boy, did we learn to do that well. If the theory that you have to spend money to make money was true, I was certainly doing my part.

Around this time, *Franchise Times* magazine came calling. Our growing roster of brands, my growing team of salespeople, and the new path we were forging for some interesting emerging franchise concepts caught the eye of this national publication. The editorial staff knew me from my Curves days, so my track record was very public. Discussing how I applied that to a stable of other brands sounded like a real page-turner. The managing editor decided to put me on the cover of the magazine. The June 2006 issue came out, and a giant photo of me with a horse greeted readers.

It was a terrific story, and it generated even more business for The Findley Group. I could not have asked for better publicity and a legitimate endorsement for the service we were providing. The industry often lived and died by the growth and strength of its franchise networks. Stories, however, could also change over time. And while that magazine cover put us on the map in a whole new way, we were also about to journey into uncharted waters. Selling franchises was one thing and entirely in our power to do well, but opening them was an altogether different matter where we had little control.

This bold experiment called The Findley Group proved razor-sharp in our ability to award deals. Unfortunately, we also got an ugly economics lesson when the time came for each brand to deliver on its promise. There was only so much we could make happen on the sales side of the business. Unlike being part of a franchisor's in-house team like our days at Curves, we no longer followed and influenced life after the sale. The Findley Group was removed from much of this equation. Operations, training, marketing support, and more were now very important functions left up to the entrepreneurs and franchise leaders. In other words, I was not the Gary Findley who would sell the deal, drive the trailer, load up the equipment, support the grand opening, and enroll new members one location at a time. Nobody at The Findley Group wore all of those hats for our clients. We simply wore the hat that brought new franchisees to a brand. The rest was up to the franchisor. Some did a great job when we handed over deals, and some did not. After The Findley Group completed the most crucial first step, we advised all of our clients about what they needed to do to carry the ball forward. It's safe to say that more than a few balls got dropped. We found the leads, qualified the prospects, and awarded franchises to people eager to join these organizations. Our clients then had to support the rest of the chain of events. That's where the rubber didn't always meet the road.

In the case of one client, I was at dinner with the founders and an investor who had brought me this deal. I could tell within minutes that their partnership wasn't working. The founders were arguing with their partner. Everyone was trying to be the boss, and that was no way to grow a large franchise network. I had built a great prototype for them, and The Findley Group was awarding tons of locations. Their operations side of the house, however, wasn't keeping pace. I saw an easy path forward. I told the investor, "Hey, if they can buy you out, you should just get out." In short, let the co-founders have it and try to run with it on their own. The founders heard this and said, "But we have no money." So, I said, "All right, I will buy out your investor, and then I'll be your partner."

Never in a million years did it cross my mind at that very moment why Gary Heavin gave me a handshake deal on my Curves earnings rather than offer me a partnership. He told me straight up that he would never do a partnership again. He had gone down that road before, only to end up in a lawsuit with that partner and then bankrupt. I was about to experience that journey for myself. I entered into a partnership with the founders of this concept, they still held a majority of the stock, and now they had the added bonus of running off their previous partner.

Somewhere in this new relationship, I was at least smart enough to have an attorney write the agreement with a buy/sell clause. Then these founders moved into my building and right under my nose. I could see they wanted to be successful, but they also had no experience running a franchise. Our relationship was strained from the beginning. I tried advising them, but after The Findley Group awarded all of these franchise agreements, the actual locations were very slow to open. Meanwhile, the mere news that these founders had reached more than 100 franchise deals simultaneously crowned them with some sort of experience they didn't really possess. The concept appeared to be a franchise sensation when, truthfully, the brand had outsourced development to a sensational sales team. Again, selling deals and opening and supporting locations were not the same thing. It was a crazy catch-22.

The icing on the cake was when the founders made a big change without telling me, a partner in their business. That was the final straw. I said we had a buy/sell clause in our partnership, and they should just buy me out. That way, they could run the company with absolutely no franchise background or experience. That sounded easy enough, right? They could have the whole enchilada and succeed or fail on their own. That's when they gave an answer I had heard before. They couldn't do it. They didn't have any money. Wait a stinking minute. What happened to the money I paid them when I bought almost half of the interest in the business? Once again, they had already spent it. Déjà vu. This was like Allen Stanford at Total Fitness all over again. What was the one lesson I learned from his personal tragedy? Never spend money quicker than you make it.

Since they couldn't buy me out, they zeroed in on their only option to gain full control of the business. It made entirely no sense, but they decided to sue me. Somehow a lawsuit was their answer to their empty pockets and total conviction that they knew how to manage a franchise organization better than me – a guy who actually had run a franchise.

It's worth pointing out that the only time I had ever been involved in a lawsuit, I did the only thing I knew how to do. I went in and told the truth, even if it didn't sit well with the guy on the opposite side of the table. Being a deposed witness for a Rainbow franchisee years ago had me going up against my former employer. Thankfully, even if there had to be a winner and a loser, both parties could appreciate me telling the truth. We all walked away, there were no hurt feelings, and I'm 100 percent sure I didn't make an enemy from the experience. What were the chances that could happen a second time? Slim to none.

This time, when it was a suit against me, I realized that people could say the craziest things and I actually had to spend time and money defending myself. They didn't have money to buy me out of the business, so they were going to drag out this legal confrontation, depose my entire staff, and let this sit in the courts forever. If there's one thing I couldn't stand, it was the inability to act. Waiting games were not my style. So I agreed to settle for a fraction of the partnership price. They only had to pay me six figures for full control of the company. In essence, I had helped to fund a franchise, assisted in designing the prototype and training center, housed the headquarters in my own building at The Findley Group, had my sales team expand the brand's national presence by awarding over 100 deals, and then went to the cleaners on my ROI. Gary Heavin was right about one thing. I could certainly see why he would never do a partnership again.

In case I hadn't see the pattern yet, I was helping to fund the creation of brands, building the prototypes, and awarding deals, only to see things fall apart on the back end when it was time to open and support these franchisees. It's too bad I didn't represent a dry-cleaning franchise. I was certainly becoming an expert on being taken to cleaners.

The third and final nail in the coffin at The Findley Group was a sweet little deal called Showcolate – a chocolate fondue concept out of Brazil. I met the founders of this kiosk chain at a franchise trade show, and they were eager to introduce their concept to North America. Brazil was among the four largest producers and consumers of chocolate in the world. This company had established some 60 locations in South America and the concept seemed awesome. From the sound of things at this franchise show, I thought it was worth a trip to see it up close.

When I arrived in Brazil, the company rolled out the red carpet for me. I toured locations and got to taste and see the business in action. The execution of the concept was a lot like an Auntie Anne's or cookie company kiosk we might see in U.S. malls. It was a small footprint with low overhead, offered easy execution for staff, and served up a truly delicious product. At these Showcolate fondue kiosks, three spinning wheels behind the glass showcased melted chocolate in three flavors: white chocolate, dark chocolate, and milk chocolate. Customers could choose from several kinds of fresh-cut fruit, and the employee at the kiosk would then dip it in the chocolate flavor of choice.

As if the presentation of the business wasn't enough, the leadership at the company took things one step further. Being very strong Christians, they prayed over everything. From the moment I arrived to talk about investing in the business until the time I boarded a plane to fly home, the rituals were overwhelming. The owner got his entire team around me and prayed over me. Then they washed my feet. Following that, they drove us up to the top of a mountain and drove a stake into the ground to signify the strong relationship we were forging together. After all of the fanfare and more than my share of chocolate-dipped fruit, we struck a deal. I gave them $750,000 to invest in the concept and bring it to the United States.

That initial investment covered the cost of manufacturing and shipping 10 of the Showcolate fondue kiosks from Brazil. The owner sent over his son-in-law to occupy an office at The Findley Group, where he would run the U.S. division we would then help grow. The tough lessons began from day one. My team at The Findley Group was successful in securing a few mall locations right off the bat. But when the kiosks arrived in the U.S., they were stuck at the U.S. Customs port of entry forever. Finally, when we gained possession of the cargo, we uncovered a serious problem. All of the materials had been manufactured according to electrical specifications for Brazil. Not a single unit had an electrical outlet that would work on U.S. soil. The lack of common sense on this project was mind-boggling. The entire inventory had to be scrapped. Once we did in fact get locations open, my investment had topped $1 million. That's when we learned the harsh reality of the American consumer and his or her all-American diet. People like to say that they want to eat healthy, but there's a dang good reason giant pretzels and cookies are all the rage at the mall instead of fruit-dipping stations. In all honesty, Americans like to go to the mall to shop and pig out. Scan any food court at the modern American mall, and you would be hard pressed to find a crowd of people saying, "I really want some fresh fruit." We drastically overestimated how the business would resonate with U.S. consumers compared to the eating habits of people in Brazil.

In rapid fashion, my $1 million investment melted away like chocolate fondue. The company dipped into that money for kiosk manufacturing (twice!), overseas shipping (twice!), and paying the very salary of the son-in-law, who now resided in my office space to manage this nightmare. If anyone needed a sweet escape, it was me from this idea. Yet, I couldn't really push this concept and the leader's son-in-law out of the country. That wasn't my redneck style. I watched this concept quietly ooze away. The son-in-law moved on when he had virtually nothing to manage. Then I contemplated how to mastermind the rest of this very predictable downfall now happening at The Findley Group.

The idea to sell deals did indeed work. The ability for franchisors (our clients) to always deliver the rest had its hurdles. I had spent the majority of the last three years and the majority of my money covering the salaries of Curves friends. Fortunately, they all had the benefit of putting experience with many more franchise brands on their resumes moving forward. Meanwhile, The Findley Group had run out of steam. If I didn't do something soon, I would be filing for bankruptcy a second time.

The one silver lining was the *Franchise Times* cover story that got me noticed. It hit newsstands when the private equity industry was taking an interest in buying franchise companies. Private equity firms, I would learn, had something in great abundance that I, on the other hand, was slowly losing: money to invest. What they didn't have was experience in franchising to determine where to park their cash. That magazine, however, introduced a guy who might be able to help.

I started getting a couple of calls from private equity firms. People were asking for my services to evaluate potential franchise acquisitions. I knew absolutely zero about mergers and acquisitions, but I also knew the well at The Findley Group was starting to run dry. I could definitely use a new source of revenue for the business. I was more than happy to consult with these firms, help them look for franchise opportunities that were for sale, and teach them what I knew about the industry.

After seeing the article, one private investor flew me to his office in Canada. He was looking to acquire Bikram Yoga, a growing network of yoga-licensed instructor businesses led by Bikram Choudhury, the founder. He wanted me to assess the organization with the idea to turn all of the licenses into franchisees. I knew a lot about fitness and a lot about franchising, but what I evaluated was more like a cult. If Bikram had one thing going for him, it was his incredible influence over his growing audience of yoga instructors. People would come from all over, pay their own way, and work for him for free for three weeks at a time to teach and license a new crop of Bikram Yoga instructors. They did all of this for the chance to say that they had worked directly with Bikram. Now, I had definitely encountered my fair share of devoted franchisees over the years, but working for free just to be a part of an organization and to get close to its founder was never a prevailing goal. I advised against trying to turn this network into a franchise, but I counted my first sneak peek into private equity investing very worthwhile. This was a whole new arena that could deliver great profits if the right deal was found.

Other private equity companies called, asking me to find them something for sale. Simply put, franchising sounded hot. What should they buy? I started doing my research for a firm and, by the grace of God, here's what happened in 2008. I phoned a growing 24/7 fitness franchise. The founder and CEO of the company was on the other end of the line. My background at Curves got his attention, and he said, "Hey, your timing is good.

I'm meeting with people next week about selling a minority share of the company." Shazam!

This guy had a mergers-and-acquisitions firm lined up, and a banker was inviting private equity companies to town. I got my investors added to the list, but we had to move quickly if we wanted a look at the action. I got back with my PE guys, and we flew to this 24/7 fitness franchise Minneapolis headquarters the very next week. The CEO was a one-man show who pitched his investment opportunity to us. He presented a PowerPoint overview of his company to us and a handful of firms. We hit it off from the very beginning. After a day of meetings, the CEO and his team spoke to their banker and said, in so many words, here is who we want you to contact. Then the banker reached out to us and said, "His exact words are, It's yours to lose.'"

That's when the attorneys got involved. The legal teams for my private equity friends and the 24/7 fitness franchise went back and forth over the negotiations again and again. They never got to a point where both parties could agree. I don't think it was an issue of price so much as how the deal was structured. That's when the CEO told his team to move on and extend the offer to another PE firm in the hunt.

The other private equity company secured the deal, and when I got the news, it was ironic. I had been in contact with them as well about franchise investments they could make. Oh well, I figured that would be the end of things as far as this franchise network and I were concerned. A day later, the CEO called. At first, I figured he was just being cordial to let me down easy. Instead, he said, "I'm going to have a new board of directors now with this new private equity deal. I'll have three seats and (the PE firm) will have two seats. I want you to have one of my three seats."

I had just chalked up a defeat with the losing team in a private equity deal, and I still won a position on the board of directors. How did that even make sense? The CEO began explaining to me that one of the reasons he tried working with my private equity friends first was to see if he could bring me on board as part of the deal. My experience at Curves was something he thought would benefit his 24/7 fitness franchise. Even though that deal fell through, he still wanted me on his team. He said, "You've been in fitness. You have the background. You know international development. So, I still want you on my board." The board position came with a little bit of stock in the company, too. Obviously, I accepted the invitation.

I flew out a little early before the first scheduled board meeting to get a closer look at the business. They had awarded some 600 franchise locations. They had ambitions to go international on a large scale. They had only one guy in-house to handle training. Nobody at the company had franchise experience outside of the concept. They had done a really good job, but I could see how they would need to step things up to support a much bigger picture. The CEO saw that, too.

The Findley Group started offering franchise development support while I offered my support on the board. Then the CEO offered me something completely unexpected in return. He offered me a job.

He wanted me to be his wingman in a C-level position and help drive things to the next level from inside the organization. He flew me and Kim to Minneapolis, met with us over breakfast, and outlined the offer. It was a good deal. It would be a newly created position. It came with a good salary. And I would get additional stock above my stock as a board member that would grow over time. Therein dangled the ultimate carrot. At the time of the most recent sale, the 24/7 fitness franchise was valued at $100 million. This was like a three-year-old company. The CEO said he wanted to double it in five years and sell off another chunk.

Private equity deals were completely next level for this old country boy. Not only was this my way to avoid a second bankruptcy, but I just might get back in the black in a huge way doing my two favorite things again: fitness and franchising. For the last three years, I had acted like a free agent for hire. I was retained by clients, I consulted for the industry, and I blew through millions of dollars in the process. A steady paycheck in two industries that I loved sounded like a pretty darn good reason to change my address. Plus, this wasn't like some of the start-ups we had been growing at The Findley Group. This was a 600-location brand that was now part of the thriving private equity frontier. If I got in at the start of this new investment, the CEO was promising some serious money when the company was sold.

He asked me for a five-year commitment in Minneapolis as an officer of the company. Considering the millions of dollars I had lost in five years and the millions of dollars I could potentially make with this, it seemed like a no-brainer. Did I forget to mention that winter hadn't arrived yet when I made my decision? I accepted the offer, and Kim hardly needed an explanation why. She hadn't liked the way I had funded The Findley Group from day one. She saw the writing on the wall. Like always, she had supported me. We gave it a good run, we expanded some brands, and then we waited for a strong return that never really came.

I had to inform everyone at The Findley Group that it was time to close up shop.

My team knew that the purse strings were getting tight. They knew I had taken care of them as long as I could. They also knew it was a pretty huge deal if this redneck was leaving Texas in order to make a living. When I shared the news about taking the job at the 24/7 fitness franchise, nobody looked shocked. At the same time, they didn't want to call it quits. The Findley Group had assembled an impressive roster of brands in three years. They told me they still wanted to make a run at things, even if I wasn't signing the checks. I didn't see the harm in that, so I sold the building and gave them all of my assets. They could have the office furniture, remain in the space, and I even paid a couple of their salaries through October. I handed over the keys and it was up to them to keep things going.

The president of The Findley Group who was now in complete control had only one request. He wanted to be the one to inform clients that the Findley behind The Findley Group was no longer a part of the company. I didn't necessarily like that, but I agreed. We all marked our calendars.

I started working for the 24/7 fitness franchise in October 2008.

The world's economy also hit rock bottom in October 2008. While I had a steady job ahead of me, the news of my departure from The Findley Group made it hard to keep those doors open. The clients ended their relationships, and the jobs drifted away. I had gone through millions of dollars in the five years after I left Curves. Now I was promising five years to a new fitness franchise in the hopes to make some of it back.

Life Lesson: Don't let your emotions drive a decision. Know exactly what is behind your decision and, above all else, always step back and take some time before making a life-changing decision.

10

MINNESOTA WINGMAN

Desperate times call for desperate measures. That saying best described my redneck life in 2008. No doubt, I was in serious financial trouble. I had left Curves in 2003 with an extra $10 million parachute. Kim and I put $2 million into our foundation for charity work. The other $8 million minus taxes – thank you, Uncle Sam – was more like $5 million. I bankrolled The Findley Group with most of that to purchase and outfit my headquarters, pay nice salaries and bonuses to my staff, and help fund start-ups and build prototypes across our client roster. The largest gamble was my $1 million investment in Showcolate that melted away to nothing. Five years was all it took to lose it all.

I would never say it was all downhill. We lived a nice life, had money to put kids through college, and worked with some amazing franchise brands along the way. Reality, however, was impossible to avoid. My bank account was on life support.

I had escaped filing a second bankruptcy by the skin of my teeth. I agreed to become a good ol' employee again right before the economy went bust. If it looked like a brilliant move on my part, then I won't say it was a nice stroke of luck. Not having so much skin in the game as a business owner somehow felt pretty good for a change. That's how I wrestled with the choice to pick up my life and willingly leave Texas for what would become five of the coldest years ahead.

I moved to Minnesota, "The North Star State," leaving behind the only place that connected with my soul. I had traveled the world by now, but Texas had always been my home. It was also where Kim and I had raised three children. Zachary now worked on a hunting ranch. Whitney had graduated from college and was beginning her career as a teacher. Micah, our youngest, was enrolled at Baylor University.

My wife and I were officially empty nesters. This was supposed to be the time of our lives, right? We could sit back, live vicariously through the accomplishments of our amazing kids, and look forward to growing old. Boy, was that a wild fantasy. Instead, we were leaving the nest right behind them. We found ourselves in a race against the clock to start over and rebuild what we had lost. As a family man, this was one of the hardest decisions I ever made. As a businessman, it was the only decision I could make.

I sold the 350 acres we had resurrected from the Camp Fire Girls. I couldn't manage the property from 1,000 miles away. I sold our motor home. I sold all kinds of things we couldn't take with us, but I kept our house. We leased our beautiful home on a golf course to a well-respected couple, who needed a place to stay while they were building a new home. Perfect timing. God willing, we would be back in five years. We stuffed our cars to the rim with the little things we couldn't live without. We corralled our dogs into the back seat and headed north. Dogs were nonnegotiable. They would go wherever this redneck went!

When we crossed into Minnesota, Mother Nature played a cruel trick on us. Winter hadn't arrived yet. The country roads throughout the state were like scenes from a postcard. I could already see us on my Harley, touring around. I even found a farmer on a tractor, stopped off, introduced myself, and offered to come and plow his fields for free on occasion. This dirt might help me reminisce about home. Hmm, maybe this whole move might not be so bad.

We got a little condo. Kim decorated the place. Then every day was an invitation to go on a scavenger hunt and find the fun in our new surroundings. At least that was the plan until winter arrived. The bone-numbing cold of the north was a rude awakening. We quickly realized, yes, we were strangers in a strange land.

Work, by the way, was a totally different kind of deep freeze. When my new boss hired me at his international 24/7 fitness franchise, apparently the C-suite role hadn't made it onto my business cards yet. I was already on the board of directors and preparing to help him run the company like he asked. Instead, he explained that I would start as the vice president of franchise development, get to know the team, and then he would promote me to run the day-to-day. What? That's not what we had discussed. I was thrown for a loop, but what choice did I have? Too bad that wasn't the only surprise.

The first day I showed up, I didn't even have an office. From the start, it was clear that the CEO hadn't told anyone I was coming. He introduced me as the head of franchising and then he arranged to have me meet with every leader across the organization. People looked at me with total surprise. He instructed team members to brief me on their divisions. Then he told me to make my suggestions for improvements as if I was already their boss. The whole thing was beyond awkward. Nobody understood why this development guy...this total stranger...this country boy with the accent...was all up in their business.

I floated around and audited the company like I was about to give a book report to the school principal. I felt utterly lost, and everyone else was equally confused. I had just moved across the country, and nobody even knew why I was there.

The very first marketing meeting I attended, the head of marketing showed off this new campaign. He was rolling it out to the entire franchise network. We're talking window clings, table tops, ceiling hangers, and more that he had supplied to some 600 locations. He didn't know me from Adam, but I pulled out two or three pieces of collateral on the table and began reading. I grabbed my pen, circled four words on the very first page, and slid the flyer back down the table. "Has this already gone out?" I asked. He said, "Yeah, why?" I said, "There are four words misspelled on there."

I had a bunch of uncomfortable introductions like this. But I brought a quick learning curve to the organization. It wasn't smooth and easy. We had five years to get things done. I had my eye on the prize, the clock was ticking, and it was time to get down to business. That was fine for the CEO's expectations. Everyone else looked like deer in headlights.

Right about this time, I got a call from a buddy back in Texas. He asked me if I had seen the national news. Our Total Fitness pal, Allen Stanford, had been arrested and indicted for using his latest company, the Stanford Financial Group, to create an elaborate Ponzi scheme. The evidence showed he had stolen some $7 billion from innocent clients who thought they were investing in CDs for a safe retirement. The TV show, "American Greed," would eventually dedicate an entire episode to Allen, calling him the Bernie Madoff of the South. A federal court in Houston found him guilty and sentenced him to 110 years in prison. I was amazed to see it all unfold. Who knew that an entrepreneur I had once admired would scheme and cheat people out of so much money to line his own pockets? The irony of that question would come back to haunt me.

Meanwhile, I kept this uncomfortable dance at the office a complete secret from Kim. It was as if I was leading a double life. As far as she needed to know, work was great and our future was back on track. In truth, I was completely faking it. I was in a strange position at work, but I couldn't walk away. A year into the job, at the company Christmas party, the CEO finally made it official and named me as his wingman in the C-suite. That went a long way to explaining why I had my hands in everything. Work actually became fun after that. In some ways, it was like reliving my days at Curves.

Despite the spiraling economy, our growth projections were strong. Franchise development deals continued. We made a successful international push. We also supported our franchisees at a much higher level. I hired a team of franchise consultant managers to assist with operations in the field. I expanded training from one lowly instructor to a department of many who could onboard new franchisees and even tackle advanced training. The company would eventually occupy a newer and bigger building to support a growing brand.

Over time, I finally found my groove.

The same could not be said for Kim. Southern hospitality didn't come naturally along the Canadian border. People in Minnesota kept to themselves. I didn't have time to mind. I was consumed with work and a fitness-and-franchise industry that I was falling in love with again. I was around people all day. I was building a team and a culture that finally started to fit our goals.

Kim, on the other hand, grew lonely. Her days were long, and the seasons were a cold backdrop to a new town with few friends. For the first year, we made it a priority to date again like high school sweethearts. We traveled on weekends throughout the state. We would hop on my Harley and ride through the countryside. We made shopping and sightseeing a regular thing. But I knew that wouldn't keep Kim busy for the next five years. She missed Texas. She missed her kids. She missed her friends. She missed our real home.

We moved into a bigger townhouse and Kim invited her friend Vicky to come and decorate the place. It was like something out of a magazine when she was finished. Kim and I loved it, and it made even the coldest days in Minnesota more comfortable.

Then our daughter, Whitney, got engaged. Hallelujah. Kim now had a very important reason to keep heading back to Texas. She had a wedding to plan, arrangements to make, and a slew of people to coordinate for the big event. Our second year in Minnesota was a commuter marriage for all the right reasons. My wife, the eternal hostess, was in her element helping Whitney arrange things. We couldn't be happier to welcome our new son-in-law, Andy, to our family. If I had written down everything I wanted in a future son-in-law, he would check off all the boxes. Kim split her time traveling back and forth, and every trip back to me was like a mini vacation. Life was good, even if it wasn't always spent together.

The inevitable big day arrived. The wedding was fantastic. Everything went off without a hitch, and we made memories to last a lifetime. Compared to the little shindig Kim and I threw to exchange our vows, this gathering was epic. I wouldn't have had it any other way for my only daughter. Of course, that made it all the harder to return back to Minnesota after the big celebration. Parties are great...until they're over. Kim counted the days for every single get-together we could arrange with the kids after that.

Eventually, Christmas rolled around. I can still remember us coming back to Minnesota after the holidays. Kim and I got back to our townhouse on a Sunday night after a great time in Texas with family and friends. On Monday morning, I woke up reenergized and ready to go back to work. When I came home, I could see the expression on Kim's face the minute I walked in the door. After you've been married as long as us, you know that look. I said, "You want to go back, don't you?" She said, "Yes." There was no doubt in my mind that she should. She quickly headed out the very next day. The fact that she lasted as long as she did in Minnesota was actually incredible, but she didn't exactly move home, either.

We had leased our house and, if nothing else, we were people with integrity. We honored our commitment to our renters. Kim moved into a 1,200-square-foot duplex that we owned in Waco even though we literally had a 4,500-square-foot house on a golf course five miles away. After the renters finished building their new house and they moved out of our home, we bit the bullet and put it up for sale. I was still years away from finishing things at my new gig, so it seemed like the best thing to do. We got a contract on it instantly. Then the buyer said he couldn't get a loan. He needed to wait until his divorce was final, so we agreed to let him lease the house instead.

Here we were, me and Kim, grown adults living like single hermits a world apart. We called these our "desert years." We were in the wilderness. Nothing was the way it was supposed to be. Kim would go out with our old friends and still feel out of place. These were husbands and wives, and Kim was their plus-one without me. I couldn't even go out to dinner with her unless plane reservations were involved. And there were many reservations to come. She would fly up for a weekend, or I would fly down for a weekend. Those frequent flyer miles became the ultimate testament to our strong marriage for the next three years.

Another guy might have thrown in the towel early and just moved back. It wasn't even up for debate. As Kim will attest, once I say I'm doing something, it's done. She might add that I'm loyal to a fault. When I gave my word, I followed through no matter how hard it became. I also tended to connect with founders. I ran their business like it was my own. It was no different at this international 24/7 fitness chain. When the CEO recruited me and I took the offer, I was in it for the long haul. We would make the private equity hawks take notice, and the trickle-down effect for the next sale would trickle a little something into my own pockets for a much brighter future.

The hardest part for me, and the saving grace for Kim, was our kids. I missed them like crazy. Even worse, I wasn't there when my grandkids were born. Kim, on the other hand, couldn't get enough of being a new grandma. While I fulfilled my obligation at work, Whitney and Andy welcomed our grandson, Wyatt, in 2010. Our granddaughter, Allie, followed in 2012. They brought a whole new level of joy to our family. They also reminded me to work that much harder to reach our goals at the fitness franchise so my exit strategy would pay off. Getting back to Texas full time couldn't come soon enough. The grandkids were my new added motivation.

The CEO and I became great friends during my time at his company. We shared a mutual goal to elevate the business and make it attractive for the next sale. When Kim moved back to Texas, I could eat, drink, and sleep work. My boss and I were constantly talking shop at the office, at lunch, at dinner, and on weekends. In no time, I was talking to him more than he was talking to his own wife. As the network continued growing, we were traveling all over the world together. We went to India, Australia, New

Zealand, Mexico, Brazil, everywhere. I was spending six days a week with the guy. I should add, this was not his style. He was not the type of guy who connected with many people at work. Before I came along, I don't think he had ever gone to lunch with another co-worker. That didn't stop this country boy from making friends and building relationships. I had his ear and, to the rest of the company, that helped to channel the team's combined goals to match his ambitions. Like me, there were a lot of stakeholders at the office who had a big payday coming their way. Everyone was working hard to get there.

After hours, if I wasn't hanging out with my boss, I played the role of lonely bachelor to perfection. I went to the mall to shop and pass time. I exercised and worked out a ton. And I ate out a lot, but mostly superfoods and clean stuff. Minnesota had healthy restaurants like Texas had churches. People lived on salads, not chicken fried steak with mashed potatoes and gravy. I was in better shape in my late 40s and early 50s than I was in high school. Meanwhile, my bride was a phone call away. And soon, very soon, we could finally be together again.

As my time at the fitness franchise was winding down, I had a townhouse in Minnesota to sell when an interested buyer came along earlier than planned. A close friend of mine wanted to have it, as is. He loved the furniture and the price was right, so we made a deal. My fallback plan was to move in with my buddy Mike. He was single, a good Christian, and the proud new homeowner of a huge house on a golf course. He had plenty of room, so he agreed to let me pay some rent for a while. Little did Kim know what this lap of luxury really looked like. Then she came to visit me and it blew her mind.

I occupied a room in the basement. Because Mike was every bit the bachelor that I said he was, he had no furniture. I had to go out and buy a bed. My previous beautiful bed was back in the fully furnished townhouse I sold. I bought plastic crates from Walmart to use as my dresser drawers for clothes. I propped a little TV on top of one, used another one as a side table, and the man-cave-on-a-budget was complete. Kim called it the most pitiful room she had ever seen. I was spending my days as an executive at a fancy office working toward a multimillion-dollar deal and spending my nights in this basement. You can bet I had hotel reservations for her stay.

As if our housing situation couldn't get much worse, our real home – that gem on the golf course back in Waco – was an unfinished transaction that had gone on far too long. We had leased our house to a man who promised to buy it as soon as his divorce was final. I guess it wasn't wise to buy a half-million-dollar house in the middle of leaving his wife. Seven months later, he was still just a renter. I had reached my limit. I called up our tenant and told him he either had to close on the house by August 1, or he needed to vacate the place. He said he couldn't afford the house. I just about died when I heard that.

He had been living in our home this whole time. Now, not only could he not afford to buy it, but Kim was in a duplex down the road and I was in a basement in Minnesota waiting for all of this to happen. I kicked him out. On August 1, the house would be empty, and Kim and I could settle down again under one roof.

I told my boss that I would finish out the last few months of my fifth year from Waco. I would fly to Minnesota regularly for the big things that needed my attention in person until the deal closed. Perhaps this was fate. Kim came to Minnesota, we rented a U-Haul and hitched it to our Escalade. We loaded the back of the SUV and the trailer with a few things we had in storage, and we headed back to Texas.

The timing was perfect for a stop in Fort Worth to see our grandkids. Whitney and Andy were having our granddaughter dedicated at their church. We got a hotel room at a La Quinta in town because they allowed dogs. Did I mention the dogs were coming home with us? Of course they were. We pulled into town on a Saturday night just in time to catch some shut-eye before the festivities. I got up early the next morning and went out to the car to get something. That's when I got a strange feeling about the sunlight coming through the windows. I opened the front door and saw shattered glass everywhere on the other side. Somebody had broken into the SUV, rifled through a mountain of possessions, and took only one thing: Kim's checkbook.

I was supposed to be at Dallas/Fort Worth International Airport in a couple of hours after the dedication at church. Kim was supposed to drive the U-Haul the rest of the way to Waco. Now I was caught up in police reports and a nightmare of check cancellations that would last several days. The culprits would ultimately land in jail after an incredible shopping spree. Having money stolen like that was a first for me, but it wouldn't be the last time I ever felt that way.

Luckily, we made it to the church. I caught my flight back to Minnesota as planned. Kim, unfortunately, was stuck driving in triple-digit heat from Fort Worth to Waco with busted-out windows. She made it back, got help unloading the trailer, returned the U-Haul, and turned in for the night. Hopefully the worst was over.

My mom called her bright and early the very next day. My parents lived in the same subdivision where our home was. She informed Kim that our tenant was having a garage sale. Wait, what? Kim knew that couldn't be true. For one thing, it was a gated community. Nobody had garage sales that people couldn't come to. And besides, it was a Monday. Who had a garage sale on a Monday? Most importantly, why was anybody even at the house? That house was supposed to be empty now.

She got in her car, the one with the busted-out windows, and drove over to our house. As her wheels rounded the corner, she could see all of the doors and windows wide open. Then as she got closer, a woman appeared at the front door with a broom. She was sweeping waves of water from inside the house out onto the front steps. Another woman sat in the garage fanning herself from the 100-degree heat. It was officially August 1, and the house was supposed to be ready for us to move back in.

Kim walked up to the women and asked, "Where's our tenant?"

They said, "Oh, he's in Bora Bora on his honeymoon." Hmm. It looked like he got that divorce finalized after all.

Kim mustered what little self-control she had left and asked, "What's going on?" They said, "Oh, the house is flooded." Somebody had left a faucet running on Friday, nobody had been there all weekend – because of the wedding and all that – and the entire first floor of our never-sold, only-rented house was completely flooded. This was the same house that the renter in Bora Bora apparently couldn't afford to buy.

The few seconds it took for Kim to get hysterical hit fast. Between violent sobs and trying to catch her breath, she blurted out, "But this is my house!"

Kim couldn't dial my number fast enough. It had only been hours since I landed in Minnesota the night before. She said, "Gary, I can't do this. The windows are shattered on my car. Our house is flooded. And the guy we told to move out is on his honeymoon."

I've never dropped things so fast. I caught the next flight back to Dallas. I was set to go to London in a few days for the rollout of the 24/7 fitness franchise in Europe. Kim was supposed to join me so we could celebrate our anniversary on the same trip. As far as I was concerned, that escape needed to happen now more than ever. The minute I got to Waco, we arranged everything with the insurance agency and immediately scheduled a restoration company to tackle more than $30,000 in damages to our home. Then, like always, Kim's friends, Glenda and Vicki, stepped in to work their magic. They took our keys, told us to keep our travel plans, and handled redecorating the entire place by the time we got back. Not only did we not sell the house, but it was more beautiful than before it was flooded. The restoration company did an amazing job, too. So much so that, after this pivotal experience, I would later pursue a career in the restoration industry. We moved back in, and Kim and I were finally together again as I waited out the last few months in our private equity journey. August was hell, but September would be heavenly. The rest of the year could only get better. Or so I thought.

I never considered myself a gifted mathematician. Then a few busted businesses, bankruptcy, and a multimillion-dollar handshake deal on a company taught me a few things. My redneck journey had polished up a few skills. My time at the 24/7 fitness franchise was a crash course in private equity funding to try and get things right from the very start.

When I took the board position at the fitness chain, I got stock. When I arrived as an employee, I got stock. Over time, I got even more stock. By the time the acquisition was on the table, I had over 3 million shares. The valuation of the company was $100 million when I arrived in 2008. The CEO said, in the next five years we would double the value and double the stock value. We were looking to hit $20 million in EBITDA (Earnings Before Interest, Tax, Depreciation, and Amortization) to get a 10-time multiple, or basically $200 million. That equated to shareholders making $1 a share. That meant my 3 million shares would pay out $3 million.

Throughout 2012, I sat through endless meetings with private equity firms looking at doing a deal. When I was still in Minnesota, I was spending half of every day with my boss on this goal alone. On top of that, we called each other at least 15 to 20 times a day. Finally, the right partner rose to the top.

The company that was going to acquire us was a private equity group out of New York City. The firm was finishing up a strong performance as owners of The Dwyer Group (now Neighborly), my old stomping grounds in Waco. It was an extremely successful investment in their portfolio, and they were looking to the franchising arena for other lucrative deals. That's when our 24/7 fitness franchise landed on their radar. The talks were incredibly positive, and my boss was confident about the numbers. The entire team at the office was preparing to celebrate, me included.

The private equity firm ended up offering $180 million for the purchase. For me, that would be shy of $3 million for my shares, but stellar overall. Throughout the negotiations, the CEO reassured everyone that they were going to double their money. Dreams were being created on the very words coming out of his mouth. Heck, one guy had already gone and bought a house with a balloon payment that was coming due. This was everyone's homerun. We were all under the same impression about the payouts that were coming our way. The marching orders were business as usual until the ink was dry.

The sale would close in December. My personal roller coaster of the last five years was about to have a beautiful ending. The holidays were going to be extra special, and the New Year was guaranteed to be happy.

Five months before the closing, we had already started transitioning for me to work from home in Texas. I would go to Minnesota a few days a week, but my base camp was in Waco. We set up everything so I could Skype calls, and my days were nonstop business as we finished the due diligence with the private equity team.

The week before the deal actually closed, I was standing in the

CEO's office. I knew we had some debt on the company, and I asked him if that would impact the $180 million. He said no. Then I repeated exactly how the numbers were supposed to look and what I should be expecting for my cut. I asked him straight up if I had it correct. He said, "Yep." There's no way we didn't get the math straight when I stood eye-to-eye and he confirmed it. That was good enough for me. It was so good, in fact, that I signed up for the next run. I told my boss I would continue on as his wingman and I would take another seat on the new board. Even during negotiations, the private equity firm asked the CEO what would happen if he got hit by a bus. He pointed to me and said, "Gary's your guy." I could see how my resume and my time at Curves satisfied such a question. So, why not stay on? I would continue working from Waco, and we would keep a great thing going.

I flew home and waited for the congratulatory news. ...And I waited. ...And I waited some more.

When the deal closed, I expected to be the CEO's first call. After all, he and I talked nonstop every day. At the very least, I expected a text. I could already see it. He would send the plane down, fly me back, and we would all go out for a huge celebratory dinner. I got no calls. I got no texts. All I heard was crickets.

It was our in-house attorney who called me on a Friday to say they finally got the deal done. Great. I thanked her and waited for my boss, my closest friend these last five years, to phone any minute. When I hadn't heard from him by Saturday, I texted him to say: "This is what we've been waiting for. I thought you would call me." He texted back and said it was anti-climactic. He only made a few million. Well, that wasn't the response I expected. I talked to him a couple of times after that, and I knew something was off. I asked him when the deal was going to get funded, and he said, "Oh, I don't know. Next week."

To hear those words from a guy who tracked every single nickel that came his way was complete hogwash. I sat on that answer and waited for the other shoe to drop. Then I got the email from our attorney with my payout. I scrolled to the bottom of the statement, and it said $320,000. Hmm, maybe that was for my stock as a board member and the rest was somewhere else. I called her and she immediately answered her phone without even saying hello. "I know. I know," she said. "I'm just as upset. I've had numerous job opportunities and I chose to stay here."

Holy crap, everyone got stiffed. She was banking on a payout of six figures. She ended up with about 10 percent of what she was expecting. The guy who had to make a balloon payment on his house called me crying. He was expecting a six-figure paycheck as well. He only got 10 percent of that, too. Instead of paying for his dream home, he was about to face foreclosure. The CEO's administrative assistant called me and said, "Oh my gosh, Gary, everybody is crying!" The entire office got news about their money on the same day. Nothing matched what their fearless leader had kept promising them right up until the very end. Even the girl at the front desk thought she was getting several thousand dollars. That would have been like winning the lottery for her. Instead, maybe she could splurge on a new set of tires for her car. The news flooded corporate headquarters like a collective punch in the gut. It was the most monumental betrayal to the most incredible group of people I've ever seen.

I kept repeating to myself: five years, five years, five years. I had left my home. I had lived apart from Kim. I had missed the births of my grandchildren. I had lost experiences I would never be able to get back because I was a man of my word. I did what I promised to do. And I felt robbed at the end. Everyone did. This deal required A.I.S. – asses in seats – in order for people to get their rewards. I knew many people at work who had received job offers to leave, but they all remained loyal in the hopes for this day to arrive. When it did, the tragedy was all too real.

The CEO was completely ambivalent about it. He acted like it was out of his hands. He might as well have said, "Oh, did I forget to tell you the deal changed a little?" The entire home office was walking around in a daze, and he brushed it all aside while he put several million dollars in his own pocket. It made me almost physically ill. He had become my single closest friend in Minnesota over the last five years, and in one fell swoop had fooled me and everyone around him who helped get him to where he was. I'm not sure what was worse: having one of my best friends tell me I would make millions of dollars only to deceive me after five years of hard work, or having a complete stranger bust out my car windows and go to town with my checking account. They both felt like criminals to me.

When the cat was out of the bag, the CEO finally Skyped me the next day. He had the nerve to say, "Hey, what's up? I heard you're pretty upset about something." I said, "What do you think?" The rest of our conversation was a textbook example on how to take five years of camaraderie and collaboration and toss them out the window. He had an excuse for everything. He explained how the exiting PE firm took its money off the top and there were fees for this and fees for that. There was nothing he could really do about it. Those were his words. That's how the deal got done. All of a sudden it was just different than the way he had told everyone – more like promised everyone – it would be. Sorry, folks. But, hey, let's all get back to work. It hit me like a ton of bricks. There was no way on God's earth that he did not know the structure of the deal when I stood in his office just days before the closing and said, "This is what we're getting. This is how it's going to work out. This is what I'm going to make." He said, "Yep."

If honesty and integrity were things I personally valued for myself, they appeared to be bargaining chips for the man who had just made millions. Up until this time in my life, I had never known mistrust on this level. Then it rolled in like a hailstorm over a wide-open Texas pasture to beat me up hard.

He had the guts to tell me that he didn't really know about the deal and what was done was done. I said, "Nobody probably knows you better than I do. Besides your wife, I know you second best. Number one, don't tell me you didn't know. Every single morning you look at your bank account. That's the kind of man you are. You did know. Number two, don't tell me that you can't do anything about it. Yes, you can. You take the front desk girl up there. This would have been life-changing money for her. It's not life-changing money for you and me, but it could be a down payment on a house to a 25-year-old girl." I told him, "You have the money. You made $40 million on the first deal, several million on this one, and you still own close to half of something that's valued at $180 million. You could put the money in there and make this right."

My advice didn't amount to a hill of beans. In the end, everyone just walked around the office crying and the founder shrugged it off. The best way to describe it is that I've never been cheated on, but that's what it felt like. It wasn't the money so much as the feeling of betrayal that I couldn't shake loose. When he had no intention of fixing things with me or any other member of his team, I couldn't stay. I couldn't trust him. I proceeded to have the worst Christmas ever. Three weeks after the sale, in January 2013, I turned in my resignation.

He called me one day and asked, "What can I do to keep you here?" I said, "Pay me my money." He said, "Here's what I'm going to do. We have a line of credit. (We, meaning him and the private equity group.) I'm going to tell these guys we need Gary to be part of the deal, so let's hit this line of credit and pay him his money."

I said, "They just gave you a $180 million value. Why would they go and put debt on a couple million dollars for an employee who has worked for you for the past five years?" Sure enough, he called me back the next day and said they didn't go for it. That was no surprise to me.

He said, "What if I offer you $5 million on the next deal, guaranteed?"

That made my blood boil. "I couldn't trust you on this one," I said. "I gave you five years of my life. I'm not going to do it again."

There's a lot of truth to that old saying: Fool me once, shame on you. Fool me twice, shame on me. No, thank you. Not ever. Not for all the money in the world.

The next several years were a quiet battleground for me. A cloud followed me everywhere I went. The aftereffects of working for and with that CEO were severe. I felt like I couldn't trust anyone. I didn't want to be with people. I didn't want to hang around friends. I wasn't even sure if my friends were the people I thought they were. My upbringing in a small town showed me how everyone looked out for one another. Now that had been ripped away. It was every man for himself.

I didn't fall into a depression so much as a deep funk. It dragged on and touched everything and everyone around me. I didn't allow myself to get close to people. I got to the point where I had so much anxiety that I decided to see a counselor and I went on medication. I even developed high blood pressure. I was secretly angry at myself for becoming a gullible puppet. But it went far deeper than that. It was a spiritual battle, and I couldn't get right with myself until I got right about how I was wronged. I went through a stubborn, uphill journey for a redneck. I had to learn the power of forgiveness. If I didn't, the actions of one man would forever have a choke hold on me. I was in my early 50s, and that was no way to live.

I prayed about this. I prayed hard. I went to my counselor as religiously as I went to church. I had helped to build business empires, but this was like climbing a much higher mountain to rebuild my soul. Finally, the day arrived when I was ready to see the CEO and tell him that I needed to forgive him. I flew to Minnesota, met with him and said my piece. It didn't even matter if he understood my need to say it. Quite honestly, he might have been baffled by it all. But in that moment, it was the freedom that I had been looking for. I didn't care to have a long conversation. I only focused on saying it to move on with my life. I also prepared myself for his response which, in many ways, was just as bad. There was no "I'm sorry it didn't work out." No "It's okay. I feel just as bad." It was utter silence and onto the next subject. That confirmed who was about to grow from the experience and who was self-inflicting an exile from ever becoming an admirable leader again. It didn't alleviate the betrayal I felt from the past, but it most certainly opened the doors to the future.

Today, I speak to men's groups about the power of forgiveness. It's important to share my journey with them in Christian organizations, business groups, and anyone on a personal level who might benefit from my lesson. We are molded to be tough. We are trained to have grit. But that doesn't mean you cannot be impacted when trust, honesty, and integrity are hugely taken for granted. That can smother a man, but it doesn't have to be his weakness. I'm proof of that, and I'm also a testament to what can flourish on the other side. I fought hard to learn the power of forgiveness in order to move on. I hope and pray that others can, too.

Life Lesson: In life you are going to have disappointments from business associates, bosses, friends, even family members. I knew, but had forgotten, this is why we don't put our trust in others or in stuff. Then I was reminded in the most heartbreaking way.

The great thing about being a Christian, however, is that God is the same yesterday, today, and tomorrow. He will never fail you or forsake you. Also, as He forgives us, we must forgive others. That's true even if it is extremely hard. Focus on the things that are important.

11

REDNECK CEO

In January 2013, Kim and I were in Cabo San Lucas on vacation. It was a trip we took every year to one of our favorite places in Mexico. We always saw celebrities there. They escaped to this exclusive resort and away from the paparazzi. This time, however, I was escaping the most brutal ending to the last five years of my career. The place was beyond upscale and incredibly private, with the price tag to show for it.

I had originally planned to go there with a couple million dollars in my pocket. But the disappointing payout from the 24/7 fitness franchise didn't keep us from having a good time. As a matter of fact, it was on this trip when I sent my letter of resignation to my boss. I was on one of the most expensive vacations and quitting my job at the very same time.

The best part of the whole trip was knowing that, after that vacation, Kim and I were headed home to the same place. For the first time in a long time, we were starting a new year back under the same roof for good. I vowed never again to commit to a job that would keep us apart. That also begged the question. What was I going to do next? I didn't have the windfall from my old job that I expected. And I certainly didn't agree to sign up for another run based on empty promises. Income, however, was a necessity. And although this may sound like a broken record, opportunities began to present themselves before I even had time to go looking.

I was on a trip in California when my phone started ringing. I was attending the HUMAN Healthy Vending conference, a franchise network run by freestyle snowboarding national champion Sean Kelly. That's when word got around that I was available to help other concepts with franchise development again. Before I had time to wallow in my misery over the previous five-year disappointment, who would have guessed it? Another fitness franchise was among the interested prospects calling me for help.

Some private equity guys I knew in Sydney, Australia, came knocking. They had a concept called EnVie Fitness with a dozen or so locations in their home country, and they wanted to bring it to America. After some conversations, I agreed to be their chief operating officer for American operations and also handle development. I went to Australia to check things out, and I liked what I saw. It was a women's-only concept, which was something I knew quite well. (By the way, did I mention that my old boss had an attorney send me a letter trying to enforce a non-compete that he told me in the beginning was just to satisfy his new partners? Let me kick you again.) I also had ideas of where and how we could bring it to the U.S. I helped the organization get the first prototype open in Texas. It would take a considerable investment from the Aussies to make an impact in key markets for a rapid launch. I was knee-deep with that plan and counseling the home office to open five or six additional corporate-owned sites when another brand came calling. And then another one reached out after that. And so on, and so on. A pattern developed practically overnight.

In the blink of an eye, I had set up shop as Findley Franchise Development and I had five concepts on my roster looking to expand. Three weeks after my resignation at the 24/7 fitness franchise, I was making more money than my old salary. Best of all, I was doing it from Texas and I wasn't financing startups, redesigns, or domestic launches with my cash. Unlike my days at The Findley Group, if a concept came to me looking to franchise, it did so with its own money. I would not — and could not — fund any more soup-to-nuts projects. Even if I had cashed out with the millions I was told to expect at my last job, I would never be the bank for other franchise brands again. I got paid for my consulting services, and it worked beautifully.

About a year into this new business, I got a call from a headhunter who wanted to introduce me to an entrepreneur in Florida named Andor Kovacs. He was an immigrant from Hungary who came to the U.S at 18 to find the American dream. He was the founder of a company called Restoration 1, and I definitely wanted that introduction. Had I not experienced a flooded house of my own, my answer may have been different. Instead, I now had firsthand knowledge and first-class respect for hard-working restoration specialists who addressed these emergencies on a daily basis. In addition, when my insurance policy paid some $30,000 in damages to the company that serviced my home, I became a huge fan of the industry and the disasters that these professionals tackled. These companies worked hard, made fantastic money, and deserved every penny. They didn't just put my home back together; they put our lives back together. As far as I was concerned, they were bonafide heroes. That one experience was all it took. I couldn't wait to meet Andor and get an inside look at this kind of business. In no time, I hopped a plane to Florida.

Restoration 1 opened in 2009, had about 26 franchise locations, and Andor was ready to take things to the next level. The business offered water damage, fire damage, and mold remediation services in a $210 billion industry. That's billion with a "b." We hit it off instantly. I could see he had his finger on the pulse of a great business with huge returns. Even better, he was delivering a service that customers desperately needed. There were no market swings that triggered an ebb and flow to this kind of operation. It was a supply-and-demand business model of epic proportions. Every busted water heater, broken pipe, hurricane aftermath, and countless other unforeseen tragedies escalated service calls to his company. I immediately saw a big future for the brand.

There were some major players in the industry, but many territories had sold out while consumer demand remained a constant. Meanwhile, these emergency services were not the type of catastrophes that homeowners wanted to wait in line to address. A little healthy competition was perfect for a new brand with a healthy bottom line, and I knew Restoration 1 could make a difference. Andor and I felt a great level of trust in each other. There was just one little catch. He wanted me to move to Florida to help him ramp things up.

Uh-oh. After my time in Minnesota, that wasn't something I was willing to negotiate. I hoped this deal wasn't dead on arrival. I told him I couldn't relocate, and I confirmed it with Kim. That was far too permanent for both of us. I relayed the news to Andor, and his reply was totally unexpected. He completely understood. He asked us to visit for six months instead. He leased a condo for us in Deerfield Beach, supplied us with a car to drive when we were in town, and told us to come to headquarters, learn the business, get to know the existing franchise network (mostly in and around Florida), and then run franchise development from Texas. It was an instant win-win. From February through December 2015, I officially served as the director of development for Restoration 1. Kim and I also enjoyed mixing work and pleasure during our time in Florida. We were a block from the beach, and every visit was like a vacation. The experience was as far from my days in Minnesota as you could imagine.

My commitment to EnVie Fitness eased up at the very same time. The Australians didn't want to bankroll the additional corporate locations, so we continued to manage the business they did have in Texas with a much lower profile or plan for expansion. To handle operations for EnVie, I recruited my sister-in-law, as well as close friend and former Curves employee, Royette, who had managed more than 400 mentors for that brand. With EnVie in good hands, I divided my time for other development clients at Findley Franchise Group and onboarded Restoration 1 to get it going. I fell in love with this particular business a little more each day.

As Kim put it, Restoration 1 did the unthinkable. Restoration became my mantra for this next phase of my life. It restored my faith in good people, a good industry, and a franchise model that was incredibly rewarding. This company was keenly focused on dirty jobs handled by professionals who were licensed and trained to do drenching, moldy, smoky, hard work. It was also about service with a smile. The individuals I got to know across the Restoration 1 network were like first responders. Every day was a dire emergency while caring for customers' most valuable assets: their homes. Similar to the experience we had with our own home, people who called up a restoration company were in a heck of a jam. The opportunity to save the day was a regular thing. On top of that, it paid well, too. Still, there was plenty of room for improvement.

Andor had seized upon a wonderful opportunity when he got into the restoration business. Like many franchisors starting out, he did amazingly well running corporate-owned locations. Nonetheless, learning to expand on that and give other people control of his brand – the franchisees who followed – was not a comfortable leap forward.

As an example, Andor had even put up some of the money to help others get into his business. These were more than franchisees to him. These were people he would socialize with, doing things together as friends. Therefore, it was none too friendly when some of these franchisees wanted to exit the system before the terms of their franchise agreements were up for renewal. In essence, these friends just stopped paying royalties. For a first-time franchisor, this is an uncomfortable position. How hard did he want to press people – guys he was close with – to uphold the legal requirements of their franchise agreements?

For me, the answer was simple. Friends or not, when the terms of the FDD are violated, that's when you go to court. That's exactly what I counseled Andor to do. We found a great franchise attorney and I told him he needed to get tough with those guys. This wasn't meant to be vindictive or overly zealous to his franchisees. Quite the opposite. It was to uphold the integrity of the contract that every other franchisee in the network diligently followed. When one person is allowed concessions or excused from following the system, it opens the floodgates for everyone else. Instead, here was the perfect opportunity to protect the brand and reinforce equal compliance for all. I advised Andor on next steps and, in doing so, I gained a whole new level of involvement with the organization. Restoration 1 won the legal battle, the unhappy franchisees were released from the system, and we focused our attention on the integrity of the brand and the bar that had been set as the network continued to grow. The experience was extremely personal for Andor, which I could understand. He and the company were stronger because of it and in a much better position going forward. That's right about the time my position going forward changed as well. Andor shared that he wanted me to do much more than franchise development for Restoration 1. He asked me to run the company.

In January 2016, I was named president of Restoration1.

This theory of Restoration 1 restoring my conviction in friends, business, and all things franchising was almost too good to be true. Here I was in a similar leadership role like at the 24/7 fitness franchise. But this time, I had a respect and trust with this founder, which I could have sworn I would never find again. I agreed to the job, but under my conditions.

I told Andor I wanted to move Restoration 1's headquarters from Florida to Waco. I wanted to build a team to support the growing network. I wanted to introduce systems to the business that were necessary to strengthen the organization far beyond just awarding franchise deals. All of this would take money. When he agreed, it was a level of respect and affirmation I had not received so unconditionally since my days at Curves with Gary and Diane Heavin. Something felt incredibly right. I wouldn't just be taking over the company. I would be investing someone else's money to do it at an astonishing level. To have his confidence spoke volumes. It also required me to rethink my other day job.

I still had Findley Franchise Development but only a couple of clients. As I started digging in as president and putting together a winning team, I eventually turned the day-to-day operations of the organization over to Todd Bingham, a fantastic business partner with a great franchising track record. Todd would manage our growing team and oversee business development, recruiting, and consulting services for our strong roster of clients, including Restoration 1 and bluefrog Plumbing + Drain. The company was rebranded to FranXperts. My sales team has always been independent contractors with the ability to sale for multiple brands. They are the best of the best, and when you eat what you kill, it drives you to work extremely hard. The organization would specialize in selling franchises that all followed a similar business model of low investment, low overhead, high margins, no brick-and-mortar requirements, and industries that were recession resistant.

With FranXperts in confident hands, I, in turn, could also fulfill my main role as president of Restoration 1 with a license to make some important decisions. When I first met with Andor, I asked him if his existing franchisees were happy. He said, yes. I asked how he knew. "Because they never call me," he explained. That wasn't the answer I wanted to hear. Having never been a franchisor, he didn't really know what to expect. And, as far as he knew, franchisees were doing well. A good franchisor, however, never waits until a franchisee calls needing something. There should be a bond from day one, which meant a franchisor won't just take someone's franchise fee and royalty payments, but also supports them in ways they couldn't on their own. That's the very essence to a good franchise system. For Restoration 1, I envisioned a chance to build remarkable loyalty by upping our game. With the right improvements, I knew we could wow existing franchisees and reengage with them in a whole new way, as well as make Restoration 1 the fastest-growing franchise in the sector. We bought a building in Waco, remodeled the space, designed a state-of-the-art training center, and then got busy.

We invested in a website redesign, a logo refresh, new uniforms, and updated vehicle wrap designs for our franchise network. I negotiated stronger relationships and better discounts with our national vendors. We hosted an annual convention to rollout our new programs. We also catapulted our franchise network in size and scope by awarding 70 deals in my very first year at the helm. I enlisted FranChoice to be our franchise brokers. They qualified franchise leads and drove them to my sales team. In return, our closing ratio set a new Restoration 1 record. Overnight, our team was awarded the Honor Roll and Master Closers awards at the national FranChoice conference. We've repeated those honors multiple times at the biannual meetings.

The excitement was electric. I started getting calls from legacy franchisees who were impressed with the changes. At the same time, new franchisees joining the network came with some amazing credentials. The revenue potential with our brand was a powerful lure to the right franchise candidates. In no time, Restoration 1 was hosting Wall Street evacuees, former Walmart execs, C-suite retirees, and more at new-owner training. These were people after my own heart. They had sharp business minds and could see the value of hard work, dirty jobs, and an incredible future helping customers nationwide.

Financially, culturally, environmentally, and spiritually, everything felt right with Restoration 1. The bottom line showed it, too. From the very first day that I met Andor, the company had no debt and took in about $800K in annual royalties. By the end of 2019, we would reach about $6 million in annual royalties. It was a leapfrog for the brand, and it sprung me into the top job as well.

The timing of my Restoration 1 journey was perfect in another rewarding way. For the first time in my career, I got to work with my son, Micah. If a fortune-teller had predicted it, neither one of us would have believed it. We certainly wouldn't have predicted how the stars would align just right. But, indeed, they did.

Micah never intended to get into franchising. And if he did, he definitely didn't see himself working with me. Who could blame him? Over the years, my family watched me travel the world to work for and with all kinds of companies. Maybe that was exciting on some level, but it was impossible to predict what I might be doing next. My kids didn't build career ambitions hitching a wagon to that.

When Micah sold his landscaping company and went to Baylor, he got a degree in management. During his senior year, he came to Minnesota and looked at a possible job as a franchise consultant for the 24/7 fitness franchise where I worked. One look at the company, and he crossed off fitness franchises from his list. The business model just didn't interest him. How ironic that fate showed me my own need to exit the business a few years later?

Instead, Micah moved to Dallas to take a job with Chase Bank. He was in the big city with a big employer and working toward a future in financing. He had a lot of fraternity buddies in town to make it all the more fun, too. But in all seriousness, the company was paying a handsome sum for Micah to sit for the Series 7 exam, a license requirement to trade stocks, mutual funds, options, and variable contracts. It was during this time at Chase Bank when The Dwyer Group (now known as Neighborly) rang him about a job as a franchise consultant with their service brand, The Grounds Guys. It was a landscaping franchise brand they were looking to grow, and Micah had been in the business, so to speak, since the ripe old age of 14. Now he had some impressive business skills to boot.

Unfortunately, the timing was bad. Micah stuck to his commitment with his employer and recommended his best friend, Jay Holland, for the job instead. Jay had worked with Micah in their landscaping business during high school, they had both graduated from Baylor, and it just so happened that Jay was working with ServiceMaster, another franchisor in the service trades industry. Not only did Jay take the job at Dwyer, but he kept Micah informed about all of the things his new employer was letting him do.

For my son, that was bittersweet. Jay was his best friend, and it sounded like he was having more fun in franchising than Micah was having in finance. Meanwhile, my son was trying to be a man of his word. That meant he stuck things out with his employer, passed the Series 7, earned his license and gave it a good run. He was incredibly smart and capable. He was also incredibly bored. After a couple of years at Chase, he knew it wasn't the kind of long-term career he wanted. So when The Grounds Guys kept growing and looked for more talent, Jay told his boss to look at Micah a second time. The next thing I knew, Micah and Jay were reunited again at a landscaping company in Waco. This time it was The Grounds Guys where Micah would serve as a franchise consultant from August 2012 until January 2016. They weren't high school kids anymore. They weren't running a business out of the back of their pickups, either. Now they were older, wiser, and helping to propel a new brand to national prominence. They were also helping The Grounds Guys become one of the fastest-growing service brands for the parent company. These kids whom I had watched grow up together were now guys with spreadsheets, P&Ls, and hands-on knowledge for managing franchisees. They saw firsthand what it took to validate the business model, support future growth, and take operations to a whole new level. The network grew from about 40 locations to 220 during Micah's time there. This was a totally different kind of learning curve than the one I received on the franchise sales side decades earlier. I harvested skills for awarding franchise deals. Micah, on the other hand, had a front-row seat on creating the tools and programs that helped franchisees perform. From training programs and vendor deals, to software and site visits, he learned how to support a rapidly growing network. Coming from different sides of the franchise business – development versus operations – Micah and I would both get baptized in franchising from our first jobs at The Dwyer Group with an invaluable level of experience.

Fast forward and, without any rhyme or reason, my introduction to Restoration 1 was a stroke of luck and destiny all at once. My very first hire was an office manager. My second hire in February 2016 was Micah. He started out as director of operations and later was promoted to vice president of operations. His friend Jay followed in May 2016 as a field consultant. Had I used a formal recruiter, I would not have found better talent. After ServiceMaster and The Dwyer Group, not to mention a few things from college, they brought operational skills to the business that I didn't have. I thoroughly knew fitness and franchising. Yet, they knew the wants and needs of the service trades. Some of that went all the way back to their high school days and the grassroots journey they made with their own landscaping company. But it went even further than all that. These were kids I had watched since childhood. They grew up together. If I knew work ethic, these boys had it. It took much more than a fancy resume, national chains, or big job titles to impress me. It went all the way back to my own days in Axtell. That's where I learned to put much more emphasis on people who understood responsibility, hard work, trust, and loyalty. That was the talent pool and company culture I was building. Even CJ Bates, my very first hire at Curves, joined the team. Familiar faces and new powerhouse industry experts rapidly converged on this new adventure. Together, we were all headed for great things.

###

The map started filling up with a slew of new Restoration 1 locations. Soon we were at 50 locations...100 locations...150...200. Things were on a roll. We also expanded the trophy case from the annual Franchise 500 rankings in Entrepreneur that we earned each year. New awards included Entrepreneur's 50 Fastest-Growing honors, Entrepreneur's Top Franchises for Veterans, and the Fast & Serious ranking of top 40 brands from Franchise Times magazine, to name a few.

Along the way, a sister company entered the picture. As our expertise in emergency services in restoration became second nature, so did the possibility of adding a second brand to the roster. That brand was bluefrog Plumbing + Drain. Headquartered in Arizona and overseen by former Dwyer Group employees, I saw a complementary business with amazing promise. Like our Restoration 1 operation, it made good sense to invest in the brand, upgrade the business systems, escalate support to the growing network, and infuse the organization with a franchise development push to take the brand to the next level. The crossover was a natural fit. In July 2017, Restoration 1 acquired bluefrog and relocated its headquarters to Waco. We became a busy dual-brand franchisor overnight.

By 2019, our growth was hardly a secret. As new agreements were being awarded, a lot of people started taking notice. That's right about the time my phone started ringing with people who wanted to talk serious money.

Private equity firms and franchise investment groups saw a solid opportunity in what we were creating. And they wanted in on the action. The experience was a bit of déjà vu. But the outcome, if I had anything to say about it, would be a whole lot different than my fitness days.

The irony of being the CEO this time around put me in control of this journey in a way I had never before experienced. I had an owner, Andor, who had given me the authority to take things to the next level. And, as fate would have it, there was an investment community that already wanted to get on the elevator for the ride up.

I started taking their phone calls. Then I started granting meetings with investors. In short order, I began to see how we might scale this great organization even faster. Over the course of a year, I had 12 companies reach out in an environment where I never made the first move. Our track record was speaking for us instead.

I made the early decision to vet each inquiry and narrow the field down to serious partners that were worth Andor's consideration. I wouldn't waste his time with every suitor until we had a serious letter of intent that was worthy of his attention and the future direction that I wanted to take the organization.

In a matter of months, I started weighing opportunities from no less than four interested investors and private equity firms. In return, they vetted a no-nonsense redneck CEO who gave it to them straight. I gave them access to my transparent team and our collective commitment to do what we do well. We all left our egos at the door and spoke frankly about the potential of what our business could mean to the right investors. We were a rapidly-growing network of brands for very solid reasons. We were expanding recession-resistant businesses. We offered opportunities with low investments and low overhead. We could train franchisees and help them open quickly. And the demand for our brands' services was never-ending. There was plenty of room to grow and plant our flags in more cities and states across the country.

Our potential dance partners in the investment arena all came with strong qualities too. They had deep pockets that offered solid financial support for the years ahead. Some even had a stable of other franchisors on their client roster. One, however, stood out from all the others.

In looking for the right partner, here's what I knew I didn't want. I didn't want a true private equity firm. I wasn't interested in a firm raising a fund with the typical buy and sell timeframe parameters that put the exit strategy above all else for the sake of its shareholders. I wanted an investment group using its own money.

I wanted the right partner with the right capital to help us build and grow while letting us do exactly what we needed to do: expand our organization with our expertise at our speed. I wanted a strategic partner that was open to acquiring additional businesses and franchise opportunities that fit our service space. And I wanted a firm I could connect with beyond the boardroom. I found all of that and more with MPK Equity Partners out of Dallas.

They were proven investors. They understood franchising. They had incredible financial strength. And they were just a short drive up the road in Dallas. The P in MPK, by the way, was for Ross Perot, Jr., a legend in the business world whose entrepreneurial father, the one-time presidential candidate, taught him well. MPK was neither the first or last firm to show acquisition interest. They were just the right firm at the right time. They came knocking midway in the pack of inquiries and from the minute I first met their team, I felt a peace in our negotiations that I had never experienced before.

MPK started getting serious with Restoration 1 in the fall of 2019. They extended a letter of interest by October. Then, much like my previous journeys with investors, there was a lot of back and forth between MPK, Andor and our leadership team to negotiate the final deal. We all saw incredible potential ahead. What we never could have forecasted was the apocalypse that awaited us and the entire world just around the corner. It was called the *coronavirus*.

As 2020 began, it looked like we were weeks away from inking the deal. My confidence about the strength of our business was never better. Restoration 1 and bluefrog Plumbing + Drain was gearing up for our biggest and best franchise convention in Vegas. Key MPK members would attend to see things up close like never before. It all went like clockwork.

And then the COVID-19 pandemic struck.

Our franchise convention turned out to be the last time many of us would board a plane and travel anywhere for quite some time. The minute we returned from our award-winning gathering, the world came to a quick and immediate stop. I had no idea what that might do to our acquisition talks.

The events that followed the COVID-19 lockdown were unbelievable. The stock market tanked. Unemployment hit record levels. The financial industry went into shock. And all of that was packaged into a presidential election year. The business community at-large took a serious blow on a global scale with the exception of a new term that would quickly become our motto: *essential business*.

Despite untold adversities, Restoration 1 and bluefrog Plumbing + Drain kept right on working. As a matter of fact, with the entire world sheltering in place, home service emergencies were all the more imperative to fix. And, likewise, a world facing a health crisis without a vaccine was equally in need of the best disinfecting and cleaning services in growing numbers. Our teams could not have been better prepared and our franchisees were nothing short of amazing in answering the call. The hazmat suits and PPP equipment that were already second-nature to our service brands and the dirty jobs our franchisees tackle year-round insured that our team members were met with a healthy dose of respect in the public's time of need.

That demand hardly went unnoticed by an investment group that was knee-deep in acquisition discussions with us for millions of dollars too. While small-businesses in other industries were closed and applying for PPP loans, our franchisees were on the front lines. And others wanted to join their ranks.

An unexpected side effect of an entire population working

remotely from home led to new franchise prospects with time on their hands to consider a career move to a more enticing career with Restoration 1 or bluefrog. I was one of the busiest CEOs in one of the weirdest times in modern history.

And in the midst of it all, was one heck of a business deal on the table.

I may have aged about eight years in eight weeks of back and forth negotiations to be acquired during the pandemic. But when the deal was funded, that first week in May was like a rebirth of epic proportions. Andor exited the company to a very comfortable retirement. In one of the most depressed economies in recent memory, he turned around and bought a Rolls Royce Phantom to mark the occasion. In return, MPK became the primary owner of our aggressively growing enterprise.

It was a nice blue-ribbon moment for this redneck too.

I got a nice piece of stock in the deal, and my role as CEO with my team moved steadily forward with a substantial partner at the table to meet and exceed our biggest goals ahead. All told, the acquisition would yield me almost exactly double what I had been falsely promised just seven years ago at a certain fitness franchise. Then we topped those projections when we added two more franchise networks, The Driveway Company and Softroc, in 2021. An umbrella company, called Stellar Brands was formed, and the rest, as they say, is history.

I would have never guessed when that deal went bust for me that I would end up here in such a harmonious position. And best of all, this acquisition has brought untold rewards to me as a person that go far beyond any monetary gain.

In short, my freedom to lead, my franchising know-how, and my trust have been restored alongside a solid work/life balance. My life and my definition of success are no longer dictated by bottom lines, but by positive experiences. That was reinforced during the pandemic when a multi-million deal ranked an easy second to the birth of two more grandchildren -- Micah's and Meighann's first daughter Emma Harper, and Zach's and Natalie's first daughter Zoe.

I have a different world view of wants and needs today that a redneck from small-town Texas could never have envisioned. My most cherished possessions are more than my bank account. I have a happy family with healthy and beautiful children and grandchildren. We have a freedom and tranquility that at one time seemed impossible to attain. I have a new personal and professional reality – I am debt free with everything in life a man could want.

And I also get to enjoy this ride of creating and expanding a portfolio of service brands to help everyone else who gets on this bandwagon with us. If ever there was a silver lining in life, this is it. The biggest bonus is the satisfaction and success I see at the grassroots level every day across our franchise networks as a result.

Today, across Restoration 1, bluefrog, The Driveway Company and Softroc we have more than 465 locations throughout the U.S., with no signs of slowing down. I'm the happiest redneck CEO as

I watch it all come together. This is as pure a business high as it gets. These brands, our team, the home office, and a sprawling franchise network across service disciplines are the ultimate reward to the aspirations this country boy from Axtell ever had. It took 60 years to get here. There have been some huge ups and some terrifying downs. However, nothing compares to the happy franchisees, the supportive home team, and the amazing family I count my blessings for today. I am that same old redneck and a renewed man, all at the same time. Life had a way of coming full circle and then launching me into the stratosphere without warning. There was a harmony to it all by doing three things all at once for the very first time in my professional career.

Today I am a franchisor. As CEO of Restoration 1, bluefrog Plumbing + Drain, The Driveway Company, and Softroc I am growing four national franchise networks and supporting them in award-winning ways.

Today I am a franchise consultant. As CEO of FranXperts, I am surrounded by incredible people who test the limits of what a brand can do to best succeed. And it's never business as usual. It provides a valuable added outside perspective that compliments those who operate within the four walls of a franchise brand.

I have also been a franchisee. I had skin in the game at the grassroots level with brands. That kept a man humble to see where the rubber met the road as opposed to the view from the corner office at corporate headquarters.

Together, these jobs keep me grounded in a way that I have never known. Like the message from "The Man in the Mirror," I am not in the rat race. I am finding what I can do with my talents to help others at every turn. I appreciate the big picture and the realities on Main Street, U.S.A. at the same time. There is peace in my life, and it shows.

Only 16 percent of U.S. franchisors have ever reached more than 100 units. It's that magical (and sometimes elusive) number that so many entrepreneurs dare to achieve. Only then can those brands claim some kind of national operational success and a growing reputation that comes with that kind of reach. I'm proud to say that I've done it a whopping six times in my career...and counting! Meanwhile, the brands I've grown and the people I've invited into those businesses have been amazing.

According to FranData, a reputable research firm for the industry, large multi-unit owners get much of the high-profile attention. But single-unit franchise owners account for more than 46 percent of the franchise market, too. That means regular people – the business owner/operators of one franchise – are an incredible part of the powerhouse behind household names and franchise brands we see every single day. Big or small, wealthy or boot strapped, urban or rural, these are the many players who make up an incredible big picture for the franchise industry and a huge economic engine for our country and, ultimately, the world.

If this is my happy ending, I'm loving every minute of it. While my success today is financially amazing, the work/life balance I have found is the ultimate pot of gold on this trail ride.

###

Remember that high school kid who wanted nothing more than to make money and buy the love of his life her dream house back in high school? He is alive and well and fulfilled in a way nobody could have foreseen.

In 2016, Kim and I sold the 27-acre ranch (purchased from Gordon) that we held onto for 18 years. It was a piece of land I had clung to since my days at Curves. It fed my small-town cowboy needs but was always shy of my forever goal. When money was tight, I couldn't let it go. When money was good, I didn't dare dream too big, either. Then, as Restoration 1 gained solid ground, I had the job title and a newfound confidence as a battle-tested redneck CEO. It was time to find my next piece of paradise. The ultimate ranch I had always imagined was somewhere out there waiting for me, and so was Kim's dream house. After months of searching farm and ranch real-estate across Texas, there were two contenders. I had Kim visit both. One ranch was more than a four-hour drive. She gave it nice remarks, but she informed me that she would never spend time there if I bought it. The place was too darn far. I couldn't argue with that.

The second ranch was about 100 acres of prime country real-estate in Stephenville, Texas, about 90 minutes from Waco. There wasn't a thing on the property that was inhabitable. But once we drove up the hill and around the bend, our eyes rested on a beautiful lake with more ducks than we had ever seen in our lives. It was perfect. Kim was in full agreement. I could already picture where we would put the house. I closed on the deal, and it was full steam ahead.

As fast as we were growing Restoration 1 and bluefrog, I was also spending every spare minute at Goose Creek Ranch. This was my name for the place and a giant work in progress. Weekends became marathons for cutting trees, hauling brush, and clearing land. We had a winding gravel road added. The crowning achievement was a brand-new barndominium. In our humble opinion, it was hands down as good as anything that Chip and Joanna Gaines had ever done on HGTV's "Fixer Upper." Kim worked with her friend Vicky to handle all of the interior decorating. The kids and grandkids all had themed bedrooms on the second floor. We added a swimming pool out back. We installed a fire pit for the best storytelling to take place for years to come. We also installed floor-to-ceiling windows across the entire back of the house with a view of the lake. It was nothing short of paradise.

My expertise zeroed in on deer blinds, electronic alerts for the front gate, and night vision cameras around the property. I know exactly when and where a critter is crossing our land or people are wanting in from the gate on the main road. The entire place has become the ultimate playground for everyone I love when the workweek is done.

In October 2018, after every painstaking detail was complete, the ranch was open for business. Furniture was in place, guests were in place, and my heart was fully healed. I don't have a proper explanation that describes how this land, my job, and my life have all come together just so, but something I was searching for all this time finally fits nicely in each and every important little way.

I've had colleagues come to the ranch instead of my office. I've hosted the company holiday party there. My family celebrated our first Christmas there in December 2018. My grandson shot his first turkey at the ranch. We've all done more than our fair share of duck hunting at the place. And I can't even begin to describe what it's like to put in a full week at the office and finish it off watching the sun go down from my back porch in the country. Goose Creek Ranch was a splurge and my ultimate happy place all at once. I don't even have to ask if my kids want to hang out with us. Sometimes my daughter, Whitney, son-in-law, Andy, and the grandkids beat us there from their home outside of Fort Worth. It's my new piece of heaven on earth, and I am truly blessed to share it with others. I see years of memories in the making that justify all the unimaginable sacrifices that Kim and I made over the years.

Whether people have faith or not, I am sure that God's hand is in all of this. And the bounty that we enjoy today is nothing short of a new beginning with the happiest of endings. His lessons and my life are a testament to what can happen with hard work, determination, and the kind of manners and respect I was raised on in a small Texas town. By His grace, I am a better person for this journey with all of its twists and turns.

That's the ultimate win for this redneck CEO. It makes for a great story. In fact, it makes great TV too.

In May of 2021, in the midst of a pandemic, I hit the road with a production crew of 20 people to begin filming an episode of "Undercover Boss" for CBS. Apparently, the story of our fastest-growing franchise, Restoration 1, combined with the essential nature of the business in the height of COVID-19 was good entertainment in the eyes of the television network. The added bonus was a boss who didn't meet the usual criteria.

Never in a million years would I have guessed a country boy from the sticks with only 24 kids in his high school graduating class would be followed around by cameras to show millions of people a day in my life. But here we were. And, boy, it was an incredible journey.

Judging from past episodes, "Undercover Boss" had featured a fair share of corner office suits over the years. These men and women were introduced to the front lines of business to roll the cameras and watch the comedy unfold. Then I came along and messed up the formula... but in a good way. When I first met the producer, he didn't hesitate to ask, "Is that what you really wear to work?" I took no offense at all. Everyone at our headquarters office could confirm that jeans, boots, and a baseball cap were my standard uniform on any given day.

A quick trip out to my ranch, and the production crew saw firsthand that I was just being myself at home and at work. I didn't mind dirty jobs, and I didn't hide behind a fancy title or a coat and tie. I was a redneck day and night and proud of it. If it meant that I didn't fit the corporate mold requirements for doing the show, I was fine with that. But, as it turned out, the network went hog-wild with my undercover character and decided it was the perfect thing to take the next level.

When I got the greenlight to be on the show, I also got the royal treatment to my undercover persona: Bobby Turner. The character that the makeup artist and wardrobe department brought to life was complete with a mullet wig, matching beard and mustache, ripped western shirt, fake tattoos and more. The redneck was in all his glory!

I had been warned that a two-week production schedule would keep me busy. Little did I know that going undercover in my own national franchise network would wear me out faster than a coyote chasing a roadrunner in a cartoon. From the minute we started filming, it was a non-stop emotional rollercoaster that could not have been more rewarding.

As one might guess, you don't go undercover on this show and not meet some amazing people with amazing stories. To see a business up close and personal in the eyes of those on the front lines who are doing the work and representing the brand every single day is transformative. And Bobby Turner saw first-hand what an incredible group of people were on the front lines of Restoration 1.

Cameras followed me from our Waco headquarters to Dallas, Washington D.C., Atlanta, Denver and back. At every stop, we also submitted to COVID testing across the entire production crew to keep everyone safe. I think back on those incredible precautions that the network took, and it only reinforces the exceptional men and women inside our business year-round who are showing up for work, doing important jobs, and serving customers no matter the dangers.

When I was paired with employees across the franchise network, I couldn't help but be humbled by their passion, their drive and their grit to succeed. Regardless of their circumstances, they all had an ability to dream. That's something a country boy knows all too well. I connected with these individuals in a way they might never fully understand. But working alongside these dedicated professionals confirmed that I am not alone in my embrace for a strong work ethic. To see others with that same dedication was beyond amazing. Their faces and our time together will remain with me forever.

I have no doubt that every single boss who has appeared on "Undercover Boss" leaves with a renewed and heightened appreciation for their organizations by seeing business through the eyes of those on the grassroots level. However, my journey also came at an epic moment in our nation's history. Our country and the world at-large was in a global pandemic. The Me Too movement and Black Lives Matter movement were all over the headlines. And the heated debate over another presidential election seemed to be rocking the country at its very core. The historical beliefs that all people are created equal, democracy is a flawless process, and opportunity in America is there for the taking were full of doubts in the national conversation. If you watched the news or scrolled social media, pride in our country and our flag seemed at a crossroads.

Who could have known that my undercover journey at Restoration 1 was the perfect medicine to restore my hope and faith in America and all that is good? Amidst the noise in our great big world, a two-week journey alongside honest and hard-working employees was the big reveal to me before my big reveal to them about our God-given gifts and the chance to do unto others. Regardless of race, gender, religion or the many other socio-economic labels we throw around, I was about to see our common thread. And it was amazing.

As expected, I had no idea who the studio was going to pair me with to go undercover in the business. At every stop, I was meeting a completely new face to experience a job up close. All of this was happening as the world's health experts shouted for social distancing and lockdowns. Timing is a beautiful thing. I was risking it all by working with people whose daily jobs involve risking it all. And here's why?

A great business requires great people. An emergency services business demands it. Our rapid growth was a sign of good times for an expanding franchise network and a redneck CEO who had found redemption in the business world. But the question remained: How do I make sure fast growth is good growth? How is the business staying the course, following the system, training great people and succeeding in the right way? A company cannot succeed only on the bottom line. Its very future depends on those who are also on the front lines.

For two weeks in May, I saw those people and, as a result, concluded without a doubt that the future is bright.

Through no master plan on my part, the network gave me a front row seat to Restoration 1 with three men and one woman as my tour guides. Every one of them was a minority. Every one of them had to work hard to succeed in life. Nothing had been handed to them. And their passion for dirty jobs at Restoration 1 franchise locations across the country was immediately clear.

No matter the destination, no matter the job, I was in costume and ready to meet a new employee for a new adventure. In every single case, we were filming from sunrise to sunset and beyond.

Along the way there was storytelling. I learned about the demands of the job. I saw firsthand that the emergency nature of this business isn't kind to family schedules, holidays, special occasions or time off. Instead, it's demanding and requires people who embrace those demands. At every turn, I saw those sacrifices as the glue that keeps it all together across our network. What these individuals do for Restoration 1 is a mere peek at what hundreds of colleagues do 24-7 across the country for the business. And to know them undercover, is to love them!

In Dallas, I met Kandeh. He was knee-deep in work related to the 2021 deep freeze across the State of Texas that resulted in the largest catastrophe insurance claims in state history. This work was also his safe haven, a job that made him crave more hours, more responsibilities and a chance for advancement. It's not every day that you see that kind of drive in a business full of dirty jobs. But it's not every day that you meet a young man like Kandeh.

Kandeh was only a child when he fled civil war in his home country of Sierre Leone. Becoming a refugee was a life or death decision. Today, however, I thank God that his life led him to Texas and to Restoration 1. The opportunities he pursued in America were proof that people not only want and need the kind of jobs Restoration 1 is growing. They also desire them with real passion. What I learned working alongside him was nothing short of amazing. Kandeh didn't have a reliable car, but he worked hard. He had lost his brother to a drunk driver, but his faith carried him through. His heart was hurting with guilt for those who never escaped Sierre Leone like he did, but his testament to them was to live an immigrant's journey with incredible resilience. My immediate desire was to honor all of those things. I was able to give Kandeh $5,000 to pursue additional restoration training and certifications that will help him advance in our industry. I gave him $20,000 to purchase a new truck. And I gifted $20,000 to the Sierre Leone War Trust for Children in his late brother's name.

His gift to me in return was showing a need across our system to create more opportunities for upward training and mobility for our dedicated and skilled technicians. I'm happy to say that is already in the works.

I then flew to Washington D.C. and worked with Tedd on a job in the suburbs of College Park, Md. My claustrophobia of small spaces was immediately put to rest when the crawl space we were working in at this home had enough room to stand. Tedd's talents to instruct, guide, smile and encourage nonstop from behind a respirator and head-to-toe Tyvek suit was all the help I needed to get through a tough, hot and messy day of wet insulation removal. The icing on the cake was meeting Tedd's pride and joy that same evening, his three daughters. A single father, you could see the love he had for those girls and his shared custody of three important futures in the making. But it wasn't lost on me that he was giving up his own bed in his one-room apartment on the days those girls were under his care.

I can still hear him telling me about his pride in his job and the ability to accomplish anything if one puts his mind to it. Fast-forward and I couldn't wait to reveal myself to this hard-working, talented service professional. I gifted Tedd the difference in rent to move his family into a two-bedroom apartment. Then I gave him $30,000 towards a college fund for his girls. Lastly, I want

Tedd to see and believe in his dream to own his own house one day. For that, I gave him $20,000 towards a down payment on a qualifying mortgage when he works, saves up and finds that perfect home for his family.

By the time I got to Atlanta, I was swept up in family stories from the front lines of Restoration 1. That's when I met Kurt, a service technician who cared for customers as if they were his own family members in need of help through a crisis. His approach to customer service was beyond my wildest dreams. And speaking of dreams, he had excelled in learning the Restoration 1 system to the point where he one day had hopes to open his own franchise.

A former graphic design artist who had lost his previous business, Kurt was not the kind of man to let life get the best of him. His love for work and for his soon-to-be fiancé were the fuel that kept him going. And I know firsthand what it's like to lose a business and start all over for the love of family, that entrepreneurial spirit, and a chance to change one's destiny.

After a service call to remove moldy baseboards in a home in Alpharetta, Georgia, Kurt and I toured the Atlanta Botanical Gardens where he shared his plans to one day propose to his girlfriend. His maturity spoke volumes as he showed me a picture of the engagement ring he had designed – a beautiful testament to his artistic skills that would not grace his fiance's hand until he could make all the payments.

When I revealed myself to him at the end of the show, I not only paid for the ring but also gave him $10,000 towards his future honeymoon. And speaking of future, I promised to cover the

$55,000 franchise fee if and when Kurt one day is ready to own and operate his own Restoration 1 franchise. In return for those gifts, I asked Kurt to share his gift for customer service with our entire system. I gave him $10,000 towards the creation of a customer service training video that will star Kurt and help Restoration 1 personnel across the country to live and lead with that same exceptional attention to detail.

Last, but not least, was the dirtiest job on my undercover journey. I flew to Denver to work with a lovely woman named Cristin who defied the stereotypes of our business by shattering any glass ceiling in her love and knowledge for her job. At Restoration 1 of West Denver, Cristin's duties as operations manager involved stocking every van for the day's service calls. She ran job estimates out in the field on a regular basis. As a professional with years upon years of experience in restoration, she even handled bio-hazard jobs that needed to be staffed. She had seen it all. Cleanup after dead bodies can be among the worst in the business, but Cristin exceeded expectations to be successful in her career and raise a child as well.

That juggling act during my visit included driving into the mountains to assess a house in Como, Colorado, where squatters had been living for 11 months with no indoor plumbing. I could smell the size of this job far before we even entered the house. Every room had been used as a bathroom. There was blood on the floor from slaughtering an animal for food. Even the camera crew had to excuse themselves from the home to get fresh air during filming. All the COVID masking got us good and ready to hold our breath for this one!

As I watched Cristin go to work identifying what her Restoration 1 team would have to remove from the home, I saw the strength of a woman in what is wrongly perceived to only be a man's world. She would later describe how hard it was to get previous employers and co-workers to take her seriously in her job. But today, working for Restoration 1, she was perfection on this job site where skilled technicians would be shuffling through the next day to demo and clean up in the very order she had laid out.

As a single mother, Cristin exuded confidence and a drive to excel. It was her hard-working illiterate parents who didn't have the luxury of finishing school that inspired her to exceed their expectations. Fast forward and she had done just that. She is proof that a woman can do more and be more regardless of the traditions in an industry. And I hope she is a shining light to others about the opportunities in restoration for all.

During my reveal to Cristin, I gave her $15,000 towards an all-expenses paid trip for her and her extended family so those hard-working retired parents could enjoy a vacation with their amazing daughter, granddaughter and soon-to-be new son-in-law. In addition, I gave her $10,000 towards the cost of her wedding. And, lastly, in the hopes that there are many more Cristins out there, I gave her $10,000 to help Restoration 1 headquarters develop a mentorship program for other women aspiring towards careers in the industry. There's plenty of room to make the service trades an equal opportunity and watch them succeed.

Going undercover in my business was beyond anything I could have imagined. As my journey ended, my entire outlook on life was expanded. I was reminded that running a business that helps others into the world of business is an incredible gift. I was reassured that job creation is alive and well, and people are thriving with those opportunities. I was forever changed by the men and woman who showed me their careers, a result of the franchise network that we continue to grow across the country. In a year of fear, angst, and uncomfortable hurdles in the world, there is a perseverance that is happening that couldn't be more comforting.

This industry has provided me with a dream-come-true feeling that I can only hope to grow for others. And I cannot thank CBS and "Undercover Boss" enough for giving validation to that mission in a time of great uncertainty for so many others. I am humbled. I am blessed. And I wake up every day with a sense of purpose unlike any other. My undercover journey may be over, but the redneck CEO is stronger than ever because of it. I love what I do, and my wish is for others to find that same harmony and reach their biggest dreams.

I often ask people what they would rather be doing if they weren't working. Do you ever get that question?

I know my answer. On any given day, I would rather be on my tractor at my ranch. It's like happiness therapy. I can instantly smell the fresh-cut grass on acres and acres in each direction under blue skies and sunshine. It's all mine. There's nothing quite like it.

Don't get me wrong. There's actual work involved in keeping a ranch in good shape, but it's the kind of work that has incredible rewards. It makes me appreciate my career that much more, because it has helped fulfill this journey.

More importantly, I think everyone deserves to find that same kind of harmony in their lives. In other words, everyone needs to find their tractor. Maybe your tractor is a lake house, a sailboat, or a week in Hawaii. Maybe your dream is to sit behind the wheel of a red Ferrari on a wide-open highway. Maybe it's college tuition for the kids. The point is, we all deserve our rewards for a job well done. When you're not in control of your career, or you don't have the financial freedom to go after your dreams, you need to rethink: What would you rather be doing instead of working?

If the job you have today will never give you the life you really want, then it shouldn't be your job tomorrow.

I've learned to make those tough calls in my own life, and it took faith, hope, and hard work to see me through. If my journey is any source of inspiration, it came with trial and error, too. My goal now is to help others see that success is always within reach. There might be obstacles along the way. There could be a boss or manager with questionable integrity. Life might kick you down more times than it lifts you up, but look for the role models. Find the mentors. Enjoy a journey of lifelong learning. Perseverance is an amazing asset for those who choose to keep tackling goals, regardless of any guarantees.

As a kid from Axtell, Texas, I wanted to be an entrepreneur. I wanted to make money. I wanted to call my own shots. I wanted to be a success. I got a taste of all of those things and more at different times over the years. Still, I somehow felt lost along the way. It wasn't until I prioritized my faith, my family, my integrity, and my willingness to help others in the right order that my career found its true home in the natural order of things. If this redneck could do it, so can you.

###

12

_____

SO YOU THINK YOU WANT A FRANCHISE

_____

Having bared my soul in this book, I've shared the highest of highs and the lowest of lows. I've made millions, lost millions, and made millions again. I've been poor and homeless, and rich... and, um, somewhat homeless, too. (Dear Texas, thank you for taking me back.)

Meanwhile, through it all, I wouldn't trade my journey for anything in the world. In fact, my journey helped me see the world. I am well-traveled and, likewise, more enthusiastic than ever about the possibilities franchising can bring to a business, and to its people – those men and women who aspire to live the dream and be their own boss in whatever franchise concept that's right for them.

That begs the question I so often receive, and it has so many different answers. When someone knows my history in this industry or, for whatever reason, trusts that I have a track record to give some kind of wisdom in return, I hear those familiar words: *Should I invest in a franchise?*

There is no universal right answer. This is not a one-size-fits-all proposition. In fact, no two franchise journeys are the same.

After hearing the Redneck CEO's story, we can agree that mine is certainly unique to me.

Nevertheless, I address this very question every day. That's especially true when I'm talking to franchise prospects for Restoration 1, bluefrog Plumbing + Drain, The Driveway Company and Softroc. (Which, by the way, is an example that has stuck with me all these decades after I saw my very first franchisor CEO, Don Dwyer, do the same with his future franchisees.) It's an invitation to dig deep and find what drives people's personal and professional aspirations. *Should I invest in a franchise?* The feedback is different for everyone, based on their current situation in life, what they want to get out of their futures, what they know or don't know about how a franchise opportunity works, and so much more. Meanwhile, the responses are the lifeblood of a thriving organization that cares for who it does and does not welcome to a franchise network for the best chance of success. Having been in this industry for several decades, I have my own thoughts.

Should I invest in a franchise? My answer is, "It depends." Franchising is not for everyone. Franchising is not a guarantee for business success. Franchising takes hard work. Franchising means following a system. Not everyone is built to walk that path. People who don't like to follow the rules shouldn't put their hard-earned money into a business system that is all about following the rules. I'm in the business of growing multiple successful franchise networks, and that means also turning people and their franchise fees away when it doesn't make sense.

Some prospects also wrongly assume that paying a franchise fee and joining a system with a well-known brand is all it takes. That couldn't be further from the truth. It takes hard work. You have to spend money before you can make money. Dedication to the brand, the system, the marketing, and training is sacred to getting that business off the ground. If anyone thinks that doesn't come with risk, they are wrong. There is incredible risk, but much less in my experience than building something from scratch. That's for dang sure what I love about franchising.

In all its glory, a good franchise is perfectly positioned to alleviate much of the guesswork for owners/operators who don't have the talent to build something from the ground up, not to mention the money it takes to make beginner's mistakes before getting something right. I know it because I've lived it.

Honestly speaking, from the very depths of my being, I believe that franchising is one of the greatest ways to do business in the world today. That comes from a country boy who has been an entrepreneur, an independent business owner, a franchisee, a franchisor, and a consultant to the franchising industry at-large. I've been on the inside and on the outside. Take it from me, being part of several successful franchise organizations can be one of the most rewarding experiences in one's professional life. On the other hand, going solo in that great, big business world can also be one of the hardest alternatives.

I know how lonely it can be operating an independent business. When you have hurdles, they're yours and yours alone. There are no peers to turn to who are in your same situation. Your successes may be sweet, but your trials may also be bitter in a life of isolation. In contrast, being part of a franchise organization is like joining a team. It delivers peers of like-minded franchisees and a collaboration to champion a brand that is powerful and purposeful through thick and thin.

Yes, it's fun to watch a brand grow from nothing to something with a national and international network. It's incredible to take a business and its products or services to all parts of the world. Additionally, after awarding more than 10,000 franchise agreements in my lifetime, there is absolutely no equal to watching others embrace and enjoy the long-held motto of franchising: being in business for yourself but not by yourself. That, in a nutshell, is the power of a franchise organization where the franchisor supports its franchisees to the fullest extent and stands by franchisees who follow the system and reap great results.

Are there failures along the way? You bet. Are there monumental successes as well? Most certainly. It's a lot like a rodeo. There will be blue-ribbon winners. There will be others who fall, get hurt, get back up, and keep on going. Not everyone is an expert on day one. But the ride is incredibly fun and rewarding for those who put in the work, train and retrain, and shine a light on the possibilities for everyone who wants to participate and be judged.

I speak from experience when I say that mentors also make a difference, and there are many in franchising to seek out. I learned from International Franchise Association Hall of Fame inductee Don Dwyer when I got my first taste of franchising. Then I learned from serial entrepreneur Gary Heavin, who was willing to risk everything on an unproven idea and grow it around the world.

I also got an ugly dose of reality when I hitched my wagon to a CEO in Minnesota who made empty promises and lost his team's faith. But it provided a lesson nonetheless. Life can be cold and lonely for those who are only in it for themselves.

However, I found an immigrant in America who showed that trust in business and in franchising could be restored, ironically with a restoration franchise. Franchising offers so many mentors, and these were just some of the important ones for me.

All of these individuals became millionaires, thanks to the wonderful world of franchising. All of them provided invaluable experiences for this kid from Axtell, Texas. I set out to make my own dreams come true and, after working with each of them, I reset my priorities higher and higher for each new step ahead. I have seen the world along the way. I have embraced a journey of lifelong learning, too. I have realized incredible wealth, and I've also lost millions. I've learned the power of forgiveness and the profound impact of giving to others. I've raised my own family while helping raise franchise families. I am the product of the American Dream, which is not an easy aspiration but a well-deserved goal for those with the same desires.

So I encourage the question for any and all who have such goals. *Should I invest in a franchise?* The answer could be life changing! Ask the question and find the mentors. If you do, your world tomorrow could absolutely exceed your dreams. Get ready for the ride of a lifetime. It has certainly been mine, and I plan on doing it until it's time for me to ride off into the sunset.

Love what you do and do what you love, and remember that you get success by hard work, honesty, integrity and, above all, learning to put others before yourself. No one cares what you know; they just want to know that you care.

Philippians 2:4 says, "Let each of you look not only to his own interests, but also to the interest of others."

That's how I want to be remembered.

Happy Trails.

###